UCLA
WOMEN'S LAW JOURNAL

VOLUME 20.1 · SPRING 2013

The UCLA Women's Law Journal is edited and produced by students of the UCLA School of Law.

Manuscripts may be submitted via email as an attachment to: WLJ@lawnet.ucla.edu or through the journal's eScholarship site at http://www.escholarship.org/uc/uclalaw/wlj

————

Please cite this issue of the UCLA Women's Law Journal as 20 UCLA Women's L.J. - (2013). Citations generally conform to A Uniform System of Citation (19th ed. 2010).

UCLA Women's Law Journal is funded by: UCLA Graduate Students Association Publications

UCLA Law School Student Bar

Cover design by William Morosi

ISSN (print):   1068-9893
ISSN (online): 1943-1708
ISBN: 978-0-9833370-7-2

————

Visit our new Open Access home at:
http://www.escholarship.org/uc/uclalaw/wlj

UCLA WOMEN'S
LAW JOURNAL

VOLUME 20.1   SPRING 2013

CONTENTS

VOLUME 20.1   SPRING 2013

ARTICLES

FOREWORD

Since its constitution over twenty years ago, the UCLA Women's Law Journal has steadfastly sought to provide a space for legal scholarship concerned with the gendered aspects of the law. We continue to publish groundbreaking scholarship on a variety of topics with the goal of demonstrating that gender issues are implicated in every area of the law.

The scholarship of this issue includes an argument for an unregulated private sperm donation market, a feminist critique of the *Citizens United v. FEC* decision, and an exploration of the application of *Planned Parenthood v. Casey* to informed consent provisions. These pieces engage the past, consider the present, and anticipate the future.

We would like to thank our brilliant and dedicated board for their hard work on this issue. In addition, we would like to thank those who are writing on topics of gender and the law and those that are advocating for women's rights. Finally, we would like to thank our readers for their continued commitment to the study women's issues in the legal arena.

MEGAN C. STANTON
CINDY Q. TRAN
Editors in Chief
UCLA Women's Law Journal
Volume 20, Issue 1

ARTICLES

THE CASE FOR AN UNREGULATED PRIVATE SPERM DONATION MARKET

Jacqueline M. Acker*

* J.D., The University of Tulsa College of Law, May 2013; B.A. The University of Texas at Austin, 2010. Many thanks to Professor Marguerite Chapman for her guidance, inspiration, and support throughout the writing process, and for sending me the article which inspired the topic of my paper. I would also like to thank Professor Sam Halabi, for being so generous with his time and advice. Thank you also to the staff at the *UCLA Women's Law Journal* for their hard work and contributions to women's issues.

1

I.   INTRODUCTION

Social networking is the new frontier for women seeking donor sperm.[1] Sperm donors and sperm-seekers with increasing frequency are meeting online, opting to forego using a sperm bank and instead choosing private donation.[2] However, the Food and Drug administration is attempting to regulate this burgeoning industry. Recently, the agency "raided the bedroom of a private sperm donor, Trent Arsenault, threatening him with jail time and a $100,000 fine for 'manufacturing' donor sperm without the proper safety checks."[3] The "safety checks" which Arsenault allegedly failed to make are based on federal regulations requiring that seven days or more before each donation, anyone who gives sperm must submit to blood tests for diseases such as HIV, hepatitis B and C, and syphilis.[4] Arsenault has donated his sperm to fifty sperm-seekers, who are mostly lesbian couples. Despite being a virgin, Arsenault

---

[1]   Tony Dokoupil, *The Coffee Shop Baby*, NEWSWEEK, Oct. 10 & 17, 2011, at 44, *available at* http://www.thedailybeast.com/newsweek/2011/10/02free-sperm-donors-and-the-women-who-want-them.html.
[2]   *Id.*
[3]   *Id.*
[4]   Erin Allday, *Sperm Donor in Fremont Feeling Heat from Feds*, S.F. CHRON., Dec. 19, 2011, http://www.sfgate.com/health/article/Sperm-donor-in-Fremont-feeling-heat-from-feds-2411681.php; *see also* Dokoupil, *supra* note 1.

has been tested at least five times in recent years, including for the abovementioned diseases.[5]

Arsenault is not the only person who may be affected by this crackdown. Another individual who could be impacted is Beth Gardner, creator of the Known Donor Registry (formerly the Free Sperm Donor Registry), which has 5,802 members.[6] This registry is an online hotspot for people seeking and donating gametes including sperm. In response to the FDA's regulation of private sperm donor Trent Arsenault, a Jane Doe plaintiff recently filed suit against the Food and Drug Administration and Health and Human Services to protect her right to receive privately donated sperm.[7]

Sperm-seekers should have the right receive privately donated sperm since there are many risks associated with sperm bank donation. For example, offspring could inherit genetic diseases or have a proclivity toward mental illness, or mothers might contract sexually transmitted infections (STI's). Also, offspring could accidentally engage in incest, or the bank might mix up the sperm and use the wrong product resulting in the creation of a genetically different child than expected. Further, legal issues may arise due to the lack of clarity regarding parental rights.

Some of the benefits of private donation as an alternative to the cryobank include the minimal financial cost, and potential access to the donor's past and future medical history and test results. The sperm-seeker or child may contact the donor if a latent genetic defect becomes apparent, and tracking donor offspring would be easier, preventing consanguinity. The sperm-seeker may meet the donor in person, and the child may have the opportunity to meet his or her biological father or potential half-siblings. The benefits of unregulated private sperm transactions outweigh the risks, which are not so substantial that they warrant an intrusion into a woman's right to choose the method of her impregnation.

This paper explores the risks and benefits of private and institutionalized sperm donation, and discusses why private sperm donation should not be regulated, allowing a woman to have the right to choose her insemination method. First, I will explain what private

---

[5] Allday, *supra* note 4; Trent Donor, *STD*, TRENT DONOR, http://trentdonor. org/std (last visited May 29, 2012).

[6] *About Known Donor Registry*, KNOWN DONOR REGISTRY, http://known-donorregistry.com/aboutkdr (last visited Apr. 10, 2012). The statistic does not only reflect sperm donors, as the Known Donor Registry also helps connect egg donors with egg seekers.

[7] Complaint, Doe v. Hamburg, et al., No. 3:12-cv-03412-EMC (N.D. Cal. filed July 2, 2012).

sperm donation is, and why it is becoming more prevalent. I will argue that a woman should have the right to choose the donor, and that a woman should have access to information about him and her children. I will investigate many of the potential risks of private and institutionalized sperm donation, including genetic diseases, STD's and STI's, consanguinity, and paternity identification. Finally, I will argue that the private gamete or sperm donation market should remain unregulated for reasons anchored in both individual liberty and the minimization of public health consequences resulting from the current institutionalized structure. As Beth Gardner said, "If it's legal to go to a bar, get drunk, and sleep with a random stranger, then it can't possibly be illegal to provide clean, healthy sperm in a cup."[8]

There are risks and benefits to private and institutionalized sperm donation. The method of sperm donation a woman chooses should be her choice, not the FDA's.

II. WHAT IS PRIVATE SPERM DONATION?

Although sperm donation for human conception dates as far back as the 18th century, acceptance of the practice has been slow.[9] It wasn't until over a hundred years later, after technology developed that allowed sperm to be frozen, that sperm donation became culturally acceptable.[10] The development of the ability to freeze sperm in the mid-20th century gave rise to the need for sperm banks, and also to vast opposition to sperm donation.[11] Some critics went so far as labeling a woman an adulterer if she used donated sperm to conceive, even if her husband consented to the procedure. Many states passed laws stating that children conceived using donated sperm were illegitimate. However, in 1965, the California Supreme Court held that children born from artificial insemination were not illegitimate.[12]

Freezing sperm was not the preferred method of storing it at first. However, factors such as the high demand for sperm, the convenience of frozen donations, and the discovery of HIV, made freezing sperm the favored storage practice by the 1980's.[13] Many

---

[8] Dokoupil, *supra* note 1 (quoting Beth Gardner).

[9] Sonia Fader, *Sperm Banking: A Reproductive Resource*, CAL. CRYO-BANK, (1993), *available at* http://www.cryobank.com/Learning-Center/Sperm-Banking-101/Sperm-Banking-History/.

[10] *Id.*

[11] *Id.*

[12] *Id.*

[13] *Id.*

professional associations discouraged the use of fresh sperm because of the risk of HIV.[14] Thanks to the development of the Internet, the face of sperm donation is changing again; today many people are opting to forgo using sperm banks, instead choosing private donation.

Private, or "directed" sperm donation occurs when a sperm donor provides his sperm to a sperm-seeker. Sperm-seekers are usually single women and lesbian couples, but they may also be heterosexual couples with fertility difficulties such as low sperm count or sterility.[15] Private sperm donation transactions are becoming more popular for several reasons. First, the financial cost is lower when compared to using a sperm bank, or "cryobank." Second, in a private transaction, donors and sperm-seekers may set their own terms regarding paternity and release of identity.[16] Persons seeking sperm donors have access to more information than ever via the Internet and can easily connect with potential donors.[17] Finally, in private transactions, potential mothers can avoid risks associated with sperm banks, and increase their chances of successful fertilization.

A. *Private Donation is Less Expensive Than Institutional Donation*

The costs of seeking donation through sperm banks are high compared to the minimal or nonexistent costs of private donation. For example, after divorcing her husband at age thirty-nine,

---

[14] *Id.* ("A year later, in response to this new threat, the American Association of Tissue Banks began discouraging the use of fresh semen among its member sperm banks. In February 1988, the American Fertility Society (now, the American Society for Reproductive Medicine), the Food and Drug Administration, and the Center for Disease Control all recommended that only frozen semen be used for DI, in conjunction with a minimum 6 month quarantine period.").

[15] Known Donor Registry, *supra* note 6.

[16] GAY AND LESBIAN PARENTING 17-18 (Deborah F. Glazer & Jack Drescher eds., 2001) (discussing both egg and sperm donors; "The question of whether to use a known or unknown donor often introduces issues related to triangulation. Among couples who have rejected the idea of having a known donor, most have stated very clearly their concern about having a third adult, and a man in particular, disrupt the equilibrium and primacy of their family constellation. A frequent worry was of jealousy and the fear that the non-biological mother would have less status than would the donor. Some couples, out of desire for the child to have a male figure in their lives, choose to use known donors. For these couples, the experience has ranged from wanting the donor to be more involved, to, less often, finding themselves in legal conflict over the rights of the various parties. In most cases, in families who do engage known donors, the choice has been a successful one.").

[17] *Id.*

Melissa's desire for children led her to search for a sperm donor.[18] She chose "Finn" from the Scandinavian Cryobank office in New York City—his sperm cost $1,250 for five vials.[19] Additionally, Melissa paid $15,000 for in vitro fertilization, hormone drugs, and doctor consultations.[20] The process was a success: Melissa is the proud mother of twin boys.[21] However, not everyone enjoys Melissa's success, nor can they afford repeat treatments. It comes as no surprise after reviewing the financial costs of Melissa's fertilization that the fertility industry in the United States is worth approximately $3.3 billion.[22]

Beth Gardner and her spouse chose a different method: directed donation. After disappointing and expensive experiences at sperm banks, Beth and her spouse sought out a sperm donor via the Internet. Frustrated with the lack of web portals for meeting sperm donors, Beth started a website, the Free Sperm Donor Registry (now known as the Known Donor Registry), which has expanded to include egg donation.[23] Through the registry, Beth and her partner found their perfect match and welcomed a baby girl on June 19, 2012 and plan on conceiving again. The registry facilitates the meeting of sperm-seekers and donors, while striving to "[e]ducate donors and recipients on safe and legal procedures, [e]ncourage Artificial Insemination (AI) over "Natural Insemination" (NI, i.e. sex), [a]dvocate for the rights of donor-conceived children, [s]trongly discourage permanently anonymous donation and parental secrecy, and [k]eep it [assisted conception] free."[24] Instead of regulating private donation, Beth Gardner proposes:

> creat[ing] a distinct set of guidelines on how to engage in private donation as safely as possible ... [which] could be as simple as recognizing private donor–recipient relationships as "intimate" and therefore exempt from the regulations governing sperm donations, or

---

[18] Mary Crane, *Sperm for Sale*, FORBES.COM, (Feb. 9, 2007, 12:00 PM), http://www.forbes.com/2007/02/09/spermbank-fertility-fda-ent-manage-cx_mc_0209bizoflovesperm.html.

[19] *Id.*

[20] *Id.*

[21] *Id.*

[22] *Id.* Due to the unregulated market for donor sperm, the figure may not be exact.

[23] Known Donor Registry, *supra* note 6. *See also* Sunny Antrim et al., *Free Sperm Site Founder Has Baby Girl, Trying for No. 2*, ABC 20/20 (Aug. 2, 2012), http://abcnews.go.com/Health/shes-client-free-sperm-site-founder-baby-girl/story?id=16905317.

[24] *Id.*

the development of some form of universal checklist or consent form that sets out each party's risks and responsibilities.[25]

Some critics of private donation worry that sperm-seekers may not have the financial resources to raise a child if they do not have the resources to pay for sperm from a bank.[26] However, many sperm-seekers are simply bound by economic circumstances. For example,[27] a young married couple that has fostered over sixty children could not have children together due to an irreversible vasectomy. Artificial insemination did not work. After finding knowndonorregistry.com, the couple began speaking with a potential donor. Both the donor and sperm-seekers are educated, nice, and loving — they are the kind of people one would expect to be exemplary parents.[28] In addition, the couple clearly has the resources to raise a child born from donated sperm when they have fostered over sixty children.

B. *Private Donation Increases the Donor Pool*

Although there are many reasons, financial and otherwise, why women might choose private donation over institutional donation, the drive for men to donate their sperm privately may not be so obvious. Donor men have cited a number of reasons, ranging from altruism, to a desire to spread their genes, to "kinky sex."[29] An example of an "altruistic" donor is Trent Arsenault, the donor whose home was raided by the FDA. Some men feel as if they are bestowing their genetics onto society as a gift. For example, one of the potential donors with whom Beth Gardner and her spouse spoke said his IQ was in the "'99.8th percentile'" ... and that he would like to "'propagate [his] genes, and help support the society of tomorrow by combating dysgenic reproductive trends.'"[30] Other donors' intentions are quite different. One potential donor said

---

[25] Lauren Vogel, *Age, Sex, Location ... Sperm Count?*, 187 CMAJ E347 (Apr. 17, 2012), *available at* http://www.ncbi.nlm.nih.gov/pmc/articles/PMC 3328535/.

[26] Editorial, *The FDA and the Sperm Donor*, L.A. TIMES, Dec. 22, 2011, http://articles.latimes.com/2011/dec/22/opinion/la-ed-sperm-20111222.

[27] Sunny Antrim et al., *From Hotel Rooms to Coffee Shops: New World of Online Sperm Donation*, ABC 20/20, Jan. 13, 2012, http://abcnews.go.com/Health/sperm-donation-hot-spots-coffee-shops-hotel-rooms/story?id-=15343381#TxXT76VWq8A.

[28] *Id.*

[29] Dokoupil, *supra* note 1.

[30] *Id.*

that he has "little interest in even a stone-cold fox if she isn't going to get pregnant," evidencing almost fetish-like intentions towards sperm donees.[31] It is these donors on whom critics of private sperm donation tend to focus.

Although the above-mentioned reasons might motivate a man to donate to a sperm bank, many donors have reservations about donating through an institution because they worry about the potential release of personal information. The anonymity they seek is not anonymity from their offspring, however; it's anonymity from the government and anyone who may use the information in an improper manner. Instead of releasing his name to an institution or agency, a private donor can reveal his identity to whomever he wants, without limitation.[32]

Other potential donors feel guilty about not participating in the lives of their biological children and wish to play a more active role in their children's lives. As refraining from such participation is often a precondition for donating to a sperm bank, these potential donors may forego donating. However, through private donation, a donor may alleviate this guilt by entering into an agreement with the donee that he may maintain a relationship with the children.

C. *The FDA's Regulatory Reach*

Recently, government regulation of sperm donation has increased. In what may be the most sensational public event that related to sperm donation, the FDA ordered Trent Arsenault, a private donor, to "cease manufacture" of sperm—the first order it had ever directed at an individual sperm donor.[33] Arsenault appealed the FDA's ruling, arguing that private donation is a form of sex, and thus, is not subject to governmental regulation.[34] Similarly, in reaction to the increase in private donor websites, Canada's public health department recently warned, "'the distribution of fresh semen [for assisted conception] is prohibited.'"[35]

D. *Women Lack Equitable Access to Institutionalized Donation*

The option to choose between private donation and institutionalized donation is essential for maintaining reproductive freedom. Throughout European and American history, the medical

---

[31] *Id.*

[32] Jamie Grifo, *A Rush to Pass Laws*, N.Y. TIMES, Sep. 13, 2011, http://www.nytimes.com/roomfordebate/2011/09/13/making-laws-about-making-babies/well-intentioned-regulators-can-harm-patients.

[33] Dokoupil, *supra* note 1.

[34] *Id.*

[35] *Id.*

profession has often dictated women's reproductive choices.[36] This trend has played out in the world of sperm donation such that some options are not available to every consumer. For example, sperm banks may choose to only allow heterosexual married women to obtain sperm, leaving lesbian couples and single women without the same number of fertility options.[37] Many insurance companies will only pay for fertility treatments if a woman can prove she has not been able to get pregnant. This policy disables lesbians and single women from obtaining insurance benefits for In Vitro Fertilization (IVF) or ART procedures.[38] In essence, a woman's reproductive freedom is limited by her lack of a male partner. In a study observing IVF, many ART professionals admitted that they would refuse to treat women who were not married or in a "long term heterosexual relationship" because they were concerned about bringing a child into a non-traditional familial relationship.[39] This limitation occurs even though lesbians and single parents compose up to 60% of the market for sperm in the United States.[40]

Discrimination in ART practices is not limited to lesbians and single women. There are discrepancies in the use of ART among women of different ethnic backgrounds in the United States.[41] Non-Hispanic white females are the most likely to use ART: they use it twice as often as Hispanic women and four

---

[36] M. M. Peterson, *Assisted Reproductive Technologies and Equity of Access Issues*, 31 J. Med. Ethics 280 (2004).

[37] *Id.*

[38] Dokoupil, *supra* note 1, at 46.

[39] Peterson, *supra*, note 36, at 282 ("Steinberg's study of attitudes held by ART medical staff found that there was a common belief that, inherent in their medical responsibilities, IVF professionals were obliged to use their 'common sense' about facilitation of 'appropriate' reproduction and in the judgment of parenting ability. The vast majority of respondents admitted that they would refuse to treat women who were neither married nor living in a long term heterosexual relationship out of concern for the potential child's need to have an appropriate family unit that included both male and female parents. This provides confirmation that many ART medical professionals feel entitled to exercise power over the reproductive autonomy of their referred potential clients, denying some women freedom of procreative choice by electing to reinforce entrenched ideologies about the family unit and sexuality.") (citing G. COREA, THE MOTHER MACHINE: REPRODUCTIVE TECHNOLOGIES FROM ARTIFICIAL INSEMINATION TO ARTIFICIAL WOMBS (1985); Deborah Lynn Steinberg, *A Most Selective Practice: The Eugenic Logic of IVF*, 20 WOMEN'S STUD. INT'L F. 33 (1997); A. Stuhmcke, *Lesbian Access to In Vitro Fertilisation*, 7 AUSTL. GAY & LESBIAN L. J. 15 (1997)).

[40] Jay Newton-Small, *Frozen Assets*, TIME, Apr. 16, 2012, at 48.

[41] Peterson, *supra* note 36.

times more often than black women.[42] The reasons for this are not completely understood.[43] Moreover, "[a]ge, income, and education level are also positively correlated with use of infertility services,"[44] although infertility rates are the highest in the lowest socioeconomic groups.[45] In essence, those with the fewest infertility problems use ART the most often. Private donation allows groups discriminated against by ART professionals to have more equitable access to resources.[46]

Women of lower socioeconomic status who are unable to afford to use a cryobank or who are turned away because of their sexuality or marital status may be fueling the private donation increase.[47] Having the option of private donation is essential for maintaining reproductive freedom and equal access to methods of conception.

E. *Technological Advancements Exacerbate this Lack of Access*

Breakthroughs in recent technology include at-home sperm tests,[48] articles dictating the best foods to consume to increase

---

[42] *Id.*

[43] *Id.*

[44] *Id.* (citing CONTEMPORARY ISSUES IN BIOETHICS (TL Beauchamp et al. eds., 5th ed., 1999)).

[45] *Id.* (citing JA Robertson, CHILDREN OF CHOICE: FREEDOM AND THE NEW REPRODUCTIVE TECHNOLOGIES (1994)). ("Lower fertility rates may be due to 'poverty, poor nutrition, and increased rates of infectious diseases and sexually transmitted diseases such as chlamydia.'")

[46] Beth Littrell, *Bias Against Gays and Lesbians*, N.Y. TIMES, Sep. 14, 2011, http://www.nytimes.com/roomfordebate/2011/09/13/making-laws-about-making-babies/fertility-industry-victimizes-gays-and-lesbians. This also helps gay men turned away from sperm donation on the basis of their sexual orientation.

[47] Peterson, *supra* note 36, at 281 ("'Procreative liberty', as defined by Robertson, is the widely accepted fundamental individual right to either have or avoid having children. This entails reproductive freedom as a negative person right, meaning that the person 'violates no moral duty in making a procreative choice and other persons have a duty not to interfere with that choice'. Thus, the ideal of 'procreative liberty' for some women often cannot be realised unless they 'qualify' of have the necessary means to access all available treatments for infertility. It is a valid interpretation to suggest that denial of procreative choice equates to denial of basic personal respect and dignity. Individuals or couples that experience infertility often experience guilt, low self esteem, disappointment, depression, increased rates of relationship conflict, and sexual dysfunction.") (citing Robertson, *supra* note 45; Luke A. Boso, *The Unjust Exclusion of Gay Sperm Donors: Litigation Strategies to End Discrimination in the Gene Pool*, 110 W. VA. L. REV. 843 (2008)).

[48] Katie Moisse, *Sperm Test to Hit Drugstore Shelves*, ABC NEWS (Feb. 8, 2012), http://abcnews.go.com/blogs/health/2012/02/07/sperm-test-to-hit-drugstore-shelves/.

male fertility,[49] and even the creation of artificial testes and viable sperm.[50] These breakthroughs all center around solving male infertility, which will help heterosexual infertile couples conceive children. As these technologies become more popular and more financially obtainable, there will be fewer infertile heterosexual couples. Thus, in the future, single women and lesbian couples will demand more sperm than heterosexual couples. However, lesbians and single women are often discriminated against by sperm banks and may not have enough supply to meet their demand due to discriminatory practices.[51] Therefore, they may be forced to turn to private donation.

F. *Fresh Sperm Increases Chance of Conception*

The likelihood of pregnancy increases when freshly ejaculated semen is used instead of cryogenically frozen sperm because the freezing process affects sperm motility and morphology.[52] However, fresh sperm may not be repeatedly tested for Sexually Transmitted Infections (STI's) and Sexually Transmitted Diseases (STD's) like frozen sperm. Therefore, many states require sperm to be frozen before use (in the context of sperm banks).[53] This practice prevents women from using fresh sperm, which would increase their chances of becoming pregnant.

III. PRIVATE DONATION AND REPRODUCTIVE FREEDOM

Women should have the right to choose the father of their child in person without having to use a sperm bank for the insemination

---

[49] Charles Bankhead, *Sperm Quality Linked to Dietary Fat*, MEDPAGE TODAY (Mar. 13, 2012), http://www.medpagetoday.com/urology/urology/31641.

[50] Rivka Borochov, *New Hope for Infertile Men*, ISR. MINISTRY OF FOREIGN AFF., Feb. 12, 2012, http://www.mfa.gov.il/MFA/InnovativeIsrael/Hope_infertile_men-Feb_2012.htm.

[51] Littrell, *supra* note 46 ("Guadalupe Benitez was denied infertility treatment by a clinic in California because she is a lesbian; the California Supreme Court ruled that the doctors' actions were illegal under the state's antidiscrimination law.").

[52] 50 AM. JUR. 2D *Trials* § 1 (1994).

[53] *Id. citing* 10 NYCRR § 52-58.5(d) (1992) ("In New York, e.g., statutory provisions require that semen specimens intended for AID be placed in labeled semen containers and kept frozen in liquid nitrogen and stored continuously in a suitable freezer reserved for semen until artificial insemination is effected. The New York scheme additionally requires that the frozen semen be quarantined for six months, and after such time, and prior to the release of the semen for artificial insemination, the donor must be retested for the HIV virus that causes AIDS, as well as evidence of other STDs.") (internal citation omitted).

process. One of the benefits of private donation is the ability to meet sperm donors in person to assess personality. Not all donors have altruistic reasons for donation, and private donation gives a potential mother the agency to screen out candidates she doesn't like.[54] After meeting privately, the donor and sperm-seeker could then use a sperm bank, although the financial costs and mistakes that sperm banks make still may deter some participants.

A. *Women Should be Able to Choose to Disclose Paternity to Their Children*

In the United States, most sperm banks guarantee donors' anonymity. However, many donors and sperm-seekers do not want the donor to remain anonymous. Allowing private donation to co-exist with anonymous institutionalized donation benefits all parties involved: women will be able to choose how much information the child will have about his or her father, donors who wish to remain anonymous may, and donors who do not wish to remain anonymous have that option as well.

Currently, no jurisdiction in the United States requires the release of donor information to donor children, although there has been a push in several other countries to allow children to gain access to donor information upon reaching maturity.[55] For example, in European countries and in Australia, laws have been enacted allowing donor-conceived children to retrieve information about their genetic fathers.[56] One purpose of these laws is to facilitate healthy familial relationships; disclosing the donor's information to the child is thought to create "open and honest communication" with children and to respect the child's autonomy.[57] Upon reaching maturity, Swedish donor-conceived children have the right to gain information about their fathers *and* to learn their identities.[58]

---

[54] Vogel, *supra* note 25, at E328 ("Many women are attracted to private donation because it allows them to meet potential sperm donors in person, and screen for personality and other characteristics that are difficult to judge from sperm bank profiles. . . . [T]he parties can also customize the level of contact they propose to maintain after a child is conceived. . . . [This] eliminates the longing to meet the donor when they're older and the child is obviously able to say 'I have a dad,' making them no different from the kids at school.") (internal quotation marks omitted).

[55] Dokoupil, *supra* note 1, at 47.

[56] Dan Gong et al., *An Overview on Ethical Issues About Sperm Donation*, 11 Asian J. Andrology 645 (2009), *available at* http://www.nature.com/aja/journal/v11/n6/full/aja200961a.html.

[57] *Id.*

[58] *Id.* (citing C. Gottlieb et al., *Disclosure of Donor Insemination to the Child:*

In Australia, practices are similar, except that the law expands to all gamete donors, and the child must either reach maturity, or an age where he or she can fully comprehend his or her decision before learning the donor's information.[59] Some programs even allow open-identity between donors and their genetic offspring due to the donor's desire to be identified.[60] A similar policy in the United States would help attain many of the goals of private donation, but it is not widely used.

Although these types of policies arguably benefit children and familial relationships, they have caused a sharp decrease in the number of sperm donors in those countries.[61] Therefore, it is harder for potential mothers to find donor sperm to create the children whom the laws were made to protect.[62] Donors dropped by 86% in anticipation of such a law in the United Kingdom.[63] The sperm-bank industry in the United States, like its European and Australian counterparts, would likely experience a drastic decrease in

---

The Impact of Swedish Legislation on Couples' Attitudes, 15 HUM. REPROD. 2052 (2000), *available at* http://humrep.oxfordjournals.org/content/15/9/2052).

[59] *Id.* (citing L. Frith et al., *UK Gamete Donors' Reflections on the Removal of Anonymity: Implications for Recruitment*, 22 HUM. REPROD.1675 (2007), *available at* http://humrep.oxfordjournals.org/content/22/6/1675).

[60] *Id.* (citing D.A. Greenfeld, *The Impact of Disclosure on Donor Gamete Participants: Donors, Intended Parents and Offspring*, 20 CURRENT OP. OBST. GYN. 265 (2008). *See also* M. Crawshaw, *Prospective Parents' Intentions Regarding Disclosure Following the Removal of Donor Anonymity*, 11 HUM. FERTILITY 95 (2008) (discussing the impact of disclosure on donor gamete participants: donors, intended parents and offspring)).

[61] *Id.* at 46 ("Many women also believe their donor-conceived children have a right to know their fathers, something most sperm banks have resisted, fearing such openness would scare off potential donors. Even banks that do reveal dads' identities will do so only when a child turns [eighteen].").

[62] Vanessa L. Pi, *Regulating Sperm Donation: Why Requiring Exposed Donation Is Not the Answer*, 16 DUKE J. GENDER L. & POL'Y 379, 380-81 (2009) ("Attention from scholars and the current international trend toward exposed donation may hasten, or at the very least trigger, a similar movement in the United States as the solution to the risks just mentioned. As Part IV will argue, the answer to the call for regulation of sperm donation is not the outright elimination of anonymity. Not only is it logical that requiring exposed donation will attract fewer donors, many countries that have taken this route have experienced varying degrees of scarcity in donated sperm. This may result in an undue burden on procreation, as well as 'fertility tourism' which would circumvent any U.S. oversight.") (citation omitted).

[63] *Id.*

donation following the implementation of donor information disclosure laws.[64]

Donations have dropped drastically in reaction to the passage of these laws because often donors want to remain anonymous. Many donors want to make money without consequences, or do not want to be involved in the lives of the children produced from their sperm.[65] Some sperm banks offer, for an additional cost, a list of donors who wish to remain in contact with their genetic offspring.[66] However, until this program is more widespread and affordable, the right of mothers to choose between a private, open transaction and the anonymity of institutionalized donation should not be precluded.

Donor information release laws and the resulting decrease in sperm donation has had an unintended consequence: sperm tourism. Women from countries where sperm donor information is released are going to other countries without these laws to obtain sperm. If similar laws were enacted in the United States, such laws could potentially ruin a multi-billion dollar industry. For this reason, private donation should not be regulated by the FDA so that it may exists as an alternative to institutionalized donation, allowing donors and donees to choose whichever process they prefer.[67]

In fact, the fertility industry in the United States is successful because of its *lack of regulation* that occurs simultaneously with over-regulation in foreign markets.[68] The lack of regulation in the United States allows for an open market where consumers dictate the market flow.[69] More regulation will likely reduce the size of the industry by limiting the availability of consumer choices that have

---

[64] Crane, *supra* note 18.

[65] *Id.*

[66] *Id.* ("To gain an edge with customers, most sperm banks were conducting these tests even before the FDA mandated them. Now, outfits like Fairfax Cryobank and California Cryobank are offering donor-consent lists containing names of donors who voluntarily agree to be contacted by their genetic offspring. [To cover the cost of tracking donors, most of these banks charge more for sperm from donors on their consent lists.]").

[67] Charles A. Sims, *A Private-Sector Problem*, N.Y. Times, Sep. 13, 2011, http://www.nytimes.com/roomfordebate/2011/09/13/making-laws-about-making-babies/the-fertility-industry-can-solve-donor-concerns.

[68] David Plotz, *Lawlessness Has Had Its Upsides*, N.Y. Times, Sep. 13, 2011, http://www.nytimes.com/roomfordebate/2011/09/13/making-laws-about-making-babies/the-lack-of-regulation-has-been-a-boon (discussing the author's perspective regarding why there is currently a lack of regulation of sperm donation generally: "Conservatives, skeptical of regulation, were glad to leave fertility alone, and let it grow into a profitable marketplace. Liberals, normally fond of regulation, were leery of doing anything to dictate women's reproductive choices. The result was an open field.").

[69] *Id.*

led to its success.[70] The United States controls 65% of the global sperm market and even exports sperm to many countries, including Venezuela, Kenya and Thailand.[71] For the market to retain its vitality, private donation must remain unregulated, especially if institutionalized donation becomes more regulated.

B. *National Registration will Solve neither Private nor Institutional Donation Problems*

Many supporters of regulation call for the creation of a national sperm donor registry, believing this will solve problems such as potential inheritance of genetic diseases, over-donation by one donor, and consanguinity. Although the registry might help tame some of these problems, it is not feasible to create an accurate and complete registry. Even if it were feasible, the consequences of the creation of a registry may outweigh the benefits.

One of the hurdles to creating national donor registries is "forging a consensus regarding content, access, privacy, and financial responsibility."[72] Currently, cryobanks have multiple policies catering to a variety of consumers. It is unlikely that they will all agree to participate in the registry if their interests are not represented. Other problems include enforcement. It would be difficult for the FDA to ensure that every sperm donor and sperm bank complied. Such a mandatory registration policy would be logistically and financially difficult to enforce, but a volunteer policy would not guarantee compliance. Moreover, if banks were required to submit donor names to the registry, it may prompt a drastic decrease in donations.

As previously illustrated, laws in Europe and Australia requiring that donors' information be revealed to donor-conceived children after they reach the age of maturity have caused a sharp decrease in the number of sperm donors. These countries import

---

[70] Recently, the world's largest sperm bank began turning down red-headed donors due to low demand. What if there was someone specifically seeking a redheaded donor? They would not have that option at that bank, and potentially would have to turn to private donation. Megan Gibson, *The World's Largest Sperm Bank is Turning Down Redheads*, TIME, Sep. 19, 2011, http://newsfeed.time.com/2011/09/19/the-worlds-largest-sperm-bank-is-turning-down-redheads/.

[71] Newton-Small, *supra* note 40, at 50 ("Thus far, sperm banking is a microcosm of a fertility industry that in the U.S. alone has expanded from $979 million in 1988 to a projected $4.3 billion in 2013.").

[72] *Id.*

more than 90% of their sperm.[73] Although donors have anonymity until their offspring reach maturity in Europe and Australia, some fear the laws to the degree that even their anticipation causes a decrease in the number of donations. The number of donors in the United States would likely decrease as well if donor information were to be collected in a national registry.

IV. PRIVATE AND INSTITUTIONAL DONATION RISKS

A. *Institutional Risks Solved by Private Donation*

The use of the wrong sperm or eggs (gametes) in insemination procedures is a risk unique to institutionalized sperm donation.[74] In some cases, the use of the wrong material is accidental; in others it is purposeful. In *Shin v. Kong*, a physician covertly inseminated a patient with his own sperm instead of the patient's husband's sperm.[75] The husband later sued the physician for intentional infliction of emotional distress after discovering that the physician was the biological father of his child. His lawsuit was not successful because the court held that the physician did not purposely inflict distress on him. This situation would be less likely to occur in private donation because fewer people would handle the material, and it would likely be used immediately as most private sperm-seekers prefer fresh sperm.

Reproductive clinics have lost or accidentally destroyed pre-embryos.[76] In a tragic case, a couple decided to conceive a child

---

[73] *Id.*

[74] Robert B. v. Susan B., 109 Cal. App. 4th 1109, 135 Cal. Rptr. 2d 785 (6th Dist. 2003), *review denied*, (Sept. 10, 2003).

[75] 50 Am. Jur. 2d *Trials* § 1 (1994) (citing Shin v. Kong, 95 Cal. Rptr. 2d 304 (Ct. App. 2000), *cert. denied* (July 19, 2000)).

[76] RESTATEMENT (SECOND) OF TORTS § 323 (1965); Jeter v. Mayo Clinic Arizona, 121 P.3d 1256 (Ariz. Ct. App. Div. 1 2005) ("Couple could sue reproductive clinic for the negligent loss or destruction of their pre-embryos under a provision of the Restatement adopted in Arizona, which applied to one who failed to exercise reasonable care after agreeing to render services to protect another's person or things; in alleging that clinic destroyed or lost five frozen pre-embryos, couple could maintain an action for harm resulting from the loss of 'things.' Couple sufficiently pled cause of action for breach of bailment against reproductive clinic in order to withstand motion to dismiss, after clinic allegedly lost or destroyed couple's pre-embryos; couple submitted three written agreements that allegedly evidenced a bailment contract between the parties, including 'consent regarding in vitro fertilization services,' 'consent regarding thawing of cryopreserved embryos,' and 'request for transfer of cryopreserved embryo or semen specimens and assumption of risk.'").

through artificial insemination before the husband succumbed to cancer. However, unreasonable storage practices by the sperm bank resulted in the wrong sperm being inseminated into the woman. The couple was surprised to find out the child did not have the husband's genetic material, and the husband died before the couple could undergo further ART procedures. The husband never lived to see the birth of his biological child due to an avoidable error.[77]

Another husband and wife suffered when a clinic failed to use the husband's sperm to fertilize the wife's eggs, and the clinic was uncertain whether the husband's sperm or wife's eggs had been accidentally given to someone else.[78] The couple worried that "they may have natural children or half children that they were unaware of, and [ ] they feared their child's natural father may someday claim rights to [the] child, thereby interfering with their rights and relationship as her parents."[79] These situations would not occur in private donation where only one person's sperm is available during the insemination process.

There are many risks for the donor, sperm-seeker (and her partner), and donor-conceived children in both private and institutional sperm transactions. There is the possibility that the sperm donor will transmit STD's and STI's to the sperm recipient, her partner, and offspring, which could lead to death.[80] Moreover, the donor could pass undisclosed genetic and/or mental diseases to the offspring. Some perils, however, are unique to procurement of sperm through an institution, including negligent semen storage,[81] increased likelihood of accidental consanguinity, or the risk of accidentally producing large numbers of offspring.[82]

B. *The Disadvantages of Institutionalized Sperm Donation*

Another force behind the popularity of private donation is the increase in information about problems in the sperm bank industry. For example, blogs, news stories, and medical studies have recently discussed the impact of sperm donation on children. Many of these sources focus on the detrimental effects and hardships that

---

[77] *Id.*

[78] *Id.* (citing Andrews v. Keltz, 15 Misc. 3d 940, 838 N.Y.S.2d 363 (Sup. 2007)).

[79] *Id.*

[80] *Id.*

[81] Newton-Small, *supra* note 40, at 52.

[82] Matthew Lee and Selcan Hacaoglu, *Italy: Libyan Opposition Will Be Recognized*, U-T SAN DIEGO (July 15, 2011), http://www.utsandiego.com/news/2011/jul/15/italy-libyan-opposition-to-be-recognized/?ap.

anonymous sperm donation may have on donor-conceived children. The increasing prevalence of this material may be augmenting the number of sperm-seekers who opt for private donation. A recent medical study found that most children born from assisted conception do not have information about their donor, even if they view their donor as their biological father and have searched for him.[83] Many of these children either support the release of the donor's identity or of detailed information about him that does not identify him by name.[84] Rachel Pepa, a blogger and cryo-baby, wrote that she has a sense of "worthlessness" knowing that her donor "sold" the genetic material that was used to conceive her.[85] If a private sperm donor had donated the sperm that helped to conceive Ms. Pepa, she might feel differently because she might know the identity of her biological father.

Recently, film, literature, and non-fiction works have touched upon the impact of ignorance about their parentage on children. The Academy Award nominated film *The Kids Are All Right* chronicles the journey of two children conceived through artificial insemination as they become acquainted with their biological father, a sperm donor. Grandparents have written testimonials about exclusion from knowing their grandchildren due to the anonymity of cryobank donation, and the loss they feel.[86] A recent feature story in the *New York Times* followed a woman who used DNA testing to search for her family after finding out she was adopted.[87]

The attention that some publicized court cases involving cryobanks receive may also cause some women to seek private

---

[83] Patricia P. Mahlstedt et al., T*he Views of Adult Offspring of Sperm Donation: Essential Feedback for the Development of Ethical Guidelines within the Practice of Assisted Reproductive Technology in the United States*, 93 FERTILITY AND STERILITY 2236, 2237-44 (2009), *available at* http://www.ncbi.nlm. nih.gov/pubmed/19285663.

[84] *Id.*

[85] Rachel Pepa, *Putting a Price on Egg and Sperm Donations*, THE GUARDIAN, Oct. 27, 2011, http://www.guardian.co.uk/lifeandstyle/2011/oct/27/egg-and-sperm-donations-price ("Did my donor care about the child he was bringing into existence or did he just want the money, which, for a medical student, would undoubtedly have come in handy? As he was anonymous it is unlikely I will ever find him and have that question answered. What I do know is, as far as I am concerned, he sold me for 15 pieces of silver—sorry, pounds —and I'm left with a big hole where a father should have been and a sense of worthlessness.").

[86] Alison Motluk, *My Scattered Grandchildren*, THE GLOBE AND MAIL (Sep. 13, 2009), http://www.theglobeandmail.com/life/family-and-relationships/my-scattered-grandchildren/article1286201/.

[87] Rachel L. Swarns, *With DNA Testing, Suddenly They Are Family*, N.Y TIMES (Jan. 23, 2012), http://www.nytimes.com/2012/01/24/us/with-dna-testing-adoptees-find-a-way-to-connect-with-family.html?pagewanted=all.

sperm donation over institutionalized donation. For example, in *Unruh-Haxton v. Regents of University of California,* the court held that the theft and sale of eggs for financial gain was not actionable because the statute of limitations had passed, and could not be tolled for intentional torts.[88] Donors want control over how their gametes and sperm are used—especially if they are used for third-party financial gain, rather than to make children. Cases like this one may cause sperm-seekers to distrust sperm banks, therefore increasing the desire for private transactions.

C. *Risks of Genetic Diseases in Institutional Donation*

Despite being regulated by the FDA, donation through a sperm bank or other institution still carries risk. Sperm carrying various genetic diseases and disorders has been sold to hundreds of women in the United States in recent years.[89] For example, in 2011, ABC News discovered "at least [twenty-four] donor-children whose father had a rare aorta defect that could potentially kill his offspring at any minute."[90] In Michigan in 2006, five children were diagnosed with a rare blood disease called severe congenital neutropenia (SCN) that requires "daily injections" to "prevent infection" and puts the children "at risk for leukemia."[91] The children all had the same father—a sperm donor who donated to the International Cryogenics sperm bank.[92] One doctor theorized that because none of the children's mothers carried SCN, the sperm donor must have been the carrier. When the sperm bank could not locate the

---

[88] Unruh-Haxton v. Regents of University of California, 76 Cal. Rptr. 3d 146 (2008); *see also* CAL. CIV. PROC. CODE § 340.5 (West 1970) ("Claims for fraud, conversion, and intentional infliction of emotional distress arising from allegations that doctors from whom plaintiffs received fertility treatments at clinic stole patients' eggs and pre-embryos and sold them for financial gain, related to wrongful intentional conduct and thus were not governed by statute of limitations in Medical Injury Compensation Reform Act (MICRA) for actions against a health care provider based upon professional negligence.").

[89] Dokoupil, *supra* note 1, at 45.

[90] Jennifer M. Vagle, *Putting the "Product" in Reproduction: The Viability of A Products Liability Action for Genetically Defective Sperm,* 38 PEPP. L. REV. 1175, 1236 (2011) (citing Denise Grady, *As the Use of Donor Sperm Increases, Secrecy Can Be a Health Hazard,* N.Y. TIMES, June 6, 2006, at F5, available at 2006 WLNR 9651819).

[91] *Id.* at 1176 ("Although SCN only affects one in five million children, there is a fifty percent chance that an affected child will pass the gene defect to future offspring.").

[92] *Id.*

father,[93] it disposed of the rest of his samples.[94] Although the bank disposed of the sperm, it did not contact the other children of the donor to inform them of the dangers of SCN, reasoning that "'even if other children had developed the disease, their families would already know it.'"[95] The donor was left without the option to release information to his children, and the children were not notified that they might be carriers of a deadly disease.[96] In contrast, some private donors, such as Trent Arsenault, a private sperm donor, readily provide their genetic records on the Internet.[97]

In another case, *Paretta v. Medical Offices for Human Reproduction*, a child was born with cystic fibrosis, a disease that must be carried by both parents to be inherited by the child. Although the sperm bank facility that Mr. and Mrs. Paretta used knew the egg donor was a carrier of cystic fibrosis, it failed to inform the plaintiffs of the donor's condition. Mr. Paretta's sperm was used in the insemination process, but his sperm was not tested for the disease. He was also a carrier for cystic fibrosis.[98] There is a similar case pending in Texas.[99]

Many of these problems might have been prevented had the donor and sperm-seekers chosen private donation. For example, the mother and donor would have been able to contact each other about any medical events. Additionally, there would not be "remaining samples" of diseased genetic material that would need to be destroyed, and the donor would be less likely to have provided sperm to create so many offspring.[100]

The tragedy in *Paretta* was that the parents were not able to contact the donor directly, but had to rely on a third party to do it for them. The Parettas relied on the bank's assurances that the

---

[93] *Id.* (The bank could not test the donor's sperm without his consent).

[94] *Id.*

[95] *Id.*

[96] Vogel, *supra* note 25, at E347. ("But interspersed among action shots of Arsenault biking in China and scuba diving in Hawaii are snapshots of his sexual health records, genetic testing results and the [fifteen] children he's fathered since hanging up a shingle in 2006 as a 'free sperm donor'.") (citations omitted).

[97] Benjamin Wallace, *The Virgin Father*, NEW YORK MAGAZINE, Feb. 5, 2012, http://nymag.com/news/features/trent-arsenault-2012-2/index5.html (providing a biography of Trent Arsenault and his journey to becoming a sperm donor).

[98] Paretta v. Med Offices for Human Reprod., 760, N.Y.S.2d 639 (N.Y. Sup. Ct. 2003).

[99] Newton-Small, *supra* note 40, at 52.

[100] Additionally, if it happened that the sperm was not only defective, but was mixed up with another man's sperm, children could continue to be born with the genetic defects.

donor did not suffer from any diseases, which was technically true since the donor was only a carrier. Had the Parettas been able to contact the donor directly instead of being forced to trust the facility's veracity, it is more likely that they would have known the donor's carrier status.[101]

D. *Risks of Genetic Diseases in Private Donation*

Private donation is not without risks. As mentioned previously, many of the risks of institutionalized donation are also present in private transactions. These include the potential that donors will transmit STD's and STI's to the recipient, donor-conceived offspring, and sexual partner(s) of the recipient, as well as the possibility that the offspring will inherit undisclosed genetic and/or mental diseases.[102]

One risk in both private and institutionalized donation is having a "rogue" sperm donor. For example, in the United Kingdom because there is a limit on the number of times a donor may donate to an institution, many men turn to private sperm donation to bypass the law.[103] Their reasons range from already having reached the maximum number of institutionalized donations to altruistic purposes.[104] Either way, some of these donors have questionable intentions and online identities–many have sexually graphic screen names and perverse motivations.[105] However, there are many donors who go out of their way to provide sperm for a cause they deem worthy, and who take steps to ensure the donation is safe.[106] A prospective mother may find comfort in having met her donor in person to assess his intentions herself.[107]

E. *The Advantages of Private Donation*

Many proponents of private donation do not believe individuals and sperm banks should be regulated under the same laws;

---

[101] DAVID ARMSTRONG, REVOLUTION AND WORLD ORDER 301-11 (1993) (emphasizing that revolutionary regimes take advantage of international law to "gain benefits" from the international system).

[102] 50 Am. Jur. 2d *Trials* § 1 (1994)·

[103] Emma John, *Conceivable Ideas: Meet the Modern Sperm Donor*, THE OBSERVER (June 26, 2010), http://www.guardian.co.uk/lifeandstyle/2010/jun/27/jennie-withers-co-parents-fertility.

[104] *Id.*

[105] *Id.*

[106] *Id.*

[107] Some sperm banks like the Fairfax bank may look at video interviews

they argue that private donors are safer. Often, people do not share as much information with their intimate partners as private sperm donors and sperm-seekers share.[108] For example, Trent Arsenault puts his blood type, genetic test results, STD test results, and sperm count online for potential donees to see.[109] If private donation becomes illegal, then sperm-seekers will be forced to rely on institutions to screen out potential donors with genetic diseases instead of seeing the results with their own eyes.[110]

If a sperm-seeker has the option to choose private donation, she will be able to choose a donor without genetic diseases. There are many publicly accessible guidelines available through which the sperm-seeker could facilitate her decision. For example, a savvy sperm-seeker may see that many guidelines require donors to provide detailed medical histories, so she could require the donor to provide his. The history could indicate a genetic disease. The power to see the medical history is important since many sperm banks do not require detailed medical histories.[111]

One sperm-seeker and her partner in Canada have experimented with both private and institutionalized donation. "She and her partner spent more than $10,000 conceiving their first child via a licensed sperm bank." When they decided to have another child, they used private sperm donation instead of institutionalized donation. They stated: "'[w]e go into it with our eyes wide open, *know what our risks are* and make the decision based on the information we're provided and what our guts tell us.'"[112] Women are capable of making their own reproductive decisions, and should have the option of continuing to do so.

Other cautions a sperm-seeker may take include requiring her sperm donor to continue to provide her with new additions to his medical history. This would be useful in the event that the donor has a latent genetic defect that was not found through initial genetic testing. After obtaining new information about his medical history

---

with sperm donors. This is a step in the right direction for institutions, but it may not be enough comfort to someone looking for the father of her children. *See* Newton-Small, *supra* note 40, at 51.

[108] Vogel, *supra* note 25.

[109] Donor, *supra* note 5.

[110] Unless the donor-seeker does not find a "private" donor and then use an institution for the transfer of the sperm. Although this is an option, it does not have the benefits of strictly private donation such as saving money.

[111] Rachel Lehmann-Haupt, *Mapping the God of Sperm,* Newsweek (Dec. 15, 2009), http://www.thedailybeast.com/newsweek/2009/12/15/mapping-the-god-of-sperm.html.

[112] Vogel, *supra* note 25, at E347.

the donor could stop providing sperm, and the sperm-seeker could take reasonable steps to protect her children from the disease. The third-party sperm bank would not control the flow of information between the donor and donee, preventing occurrences like the severe congenital neutropenia case in Michigan where the bank refused to tell the donor's children about their father's genetic defect.

Another cheap method to screen sperm donors, private and institutionalized, is to require prospective donors to complete a detailed family history. This method may be effective in preventing the use of sperm from those predisposed to passing on genetic disorders.[113] Donors (and sperm-seekers) may opt to get one comprehensive genetic screening test in their lifetime. In the near future, hopefully between 2016 and 2017, a complete genetic sequencing test may be done for less than $1,000.[114] This information can then be available to sperm-seekers. These genetic tests could be more useful than the current medical history report for detecting genetic diseases.[115]

Some sperm donors, like Arsenault, put all of their medical test results and personal information on display, *and* practice celibacy. A Canadian student who is a free sperm donor has

> taken greater precautions in preparing to become a private donor than even most recipients require. In addition to screening for sexually-transmitted infections, he has undergone genetic testing, conferred with a lawyer about his responsibilities to recipients and any resulting children, and sought to determine whether there is a maximum number of children a donor may have per population. And like Arsenault, [he] abstains from sex.[116]

Another option available to the sperm-seeker is to ask for a comprehensive genetic questionnaire to be completed.[117] These

---

[113] Robert G. Brzyski, *Start with Some Hard Questions*, N.Y. TIMES, Sep. 13, 2011, *available at* http://www.nytimes.com/roomfordebate/2011/09/13/making-laws-about-making-babies/before-regulation-the-fertility-industry-some-hard-questions.

[114] CRACKING YOUR GENETIC CODE (PBS television broadcast Mar. 28, 2012), *available at* http://www.pbs.org/wgbh/nova/body/cracking-your-genetic-code.html.

[115] U.S. DEP'T OF ENERGY, GENE TESTING (2010), *available at* http://www.ornl.gov/sci/techresources/Human_Genome/medicine/genetest.shtml#testsavailable.

[116] Vogel, *supra* note 25.

[117] There is the risk that the donor does not know his genetic history, or does

questionnaires may provide equal insight to the risk for some genetic diseases since many are inheritable.[118]

One Court alluded to the benefits of sperm bank deregula-
tion, reasoning that because the sciences of reproductive technologies are constantly in flux and improving, banks should not become
totally regulated.[119] However, the court said that instead of full de-
regulation, the system should allow both private and institutionalized donation.

V. STD and STI Risk in Institutionalized and Private Donation

A. *Current Regulations*

There are laws in many states that regulate the testing of
sperm and sperm donors for STD's and STI's. For example, Oklahoma requires the sperm and/or donor to be tested before insemination, and it is illegal to donate sperm, or to procure it if the donor
tests positive for HIV.[120]

B. *STD and STI Risk in Institutionalized Donation*

Some institutions, *but not all*, test both the donor and the
sperm for STD's and STI's.[121] Truly, "there is little uniformity among
sperm banks as to the screening practices they employ to determine

---

not list every known disorder.

[118] Yaniv Heled, *The Regulation of Genetic Aspects of Donated Reproductive Tissue-the Need for Federal Regulation*, 11 COLUM. SCI. & TECH. L. REV. 243,
270-72 (2010), *quoting* AM. ASS'N OF TISSUE BANKS, STANDARDS FOR TISSUE
BANKING (10th ed. 2002) [hereinafter *AATB Guidelines*] (According to the
AATB, donors who have family members or themselves have any condition
which could pose a risk of genetic diseases "greater than the risk in the general
population," should be disqualified. The Guidelines state that if there is a risk
of "Tay-Sachs disease, thalassemia, sickle cell anemia or CF in the donor's medical history, family history or ethnic background, the donor should be tested for
such conditions.").

[119] Ferguson v. McKiernan, 940 A.2d 1236, 1248 (2007) ("The absence of
a legislative mandate coupled to the constantly evolving science of reproductive technology and the other considerations highlighted above illustrate the
very opposite of unanimity with regard to the legal relationships arising from
sperm donation, whether anonymous or otherwise. This undermines any sug-
gestion that the agreement at issue violates a 'dominant public policy' or 'obvious ethical or moral standards' (citations omitted) sufficient to warrant the
invalidation of an otherwise binding agreement.")·

[120] Okla. Stat. Ann. tit. 63, § 2151.1 (West 1988).

[121] 50 Am. Jur. 2d *Trials* § 1 (1994).

the acceptability of semen to be used for artificial insemination."[122] There are no uniform laws regulating sperm banks, and many of the laws that are in place are unclear.[123] This is problematic for a sperm-seeker who relies on the institution to comprehensively test the donor and/or donor sperm for disease and does not conduct her own investigation.

C. *STD & STI Risks and Benefits Common to both Private and Institutionalized Donation*

Some institutions use questionnaires to screen donors based on their past sexual history, drug use, and more before spending money on testing for disease.[124] This same process could be accomplished by private sperm-seekers to narrow down the pool of potential donors, thereby preventing unnecessary testing expenditures. The downside to relying on these questionnaires is that the donee is reliant on the donor's truthfulness or awareness of his medical status.[125] However, if used properly as the first step in screening potential donors, and in addition to actual testing, this process would effectively screen out some infected donors.[126]

Although the risk of dishonesty applies to all types of donation practices, in private, free donation transactions the donor does not have a financial incentive to lie. Most, if not all, private sperm donors do not sell their sperm, they provide it for free, whereas a male donating to a sperm bank may make up to $500 per expulsion. Potentially, such a donor could make about $30,000 a year.

---

[122] *Id.*

[123] *Id.*

[124] *Id.*

[125] Heled, *supra* note 118, at 277-78 ("Moreover, the current scheme of self-regulation relies primarily on the diligence and integrity of practitioners as well as on donors volunteering pertinent information about their medical history and that of their families. However, practitioners operate in a highly competitive market that creates strong financial incentives that do not necessarily coincide with the best interest of DRT recipients and DRT children. Potential donors' answers regarding their medical history and that of their families are also often insufficient to properly evaluate the genetic risks they might pose. Furthermore, the financial benefit to donors accompanied by the absence of a clear legal duty to accurately disclose such information might render the current screening practices — which rely mostly on questioning of potential donors — unreliable because they create an incentive for potential donors to hide negative medical facts about themselves and their families. As a result, a significant number of the many thousands of children born every year from DRT are exposed to a heightened risk of having severe genetic diseases which could have been avoided through proper genetic screening.") (citations omitted).

[126] *Id.* at 267-70.

A college graduate may make at least $60 per ejaculate.[127] It is unlikely that a donor would be so bashful that he would not disclose his purposes for donating to a sperm-seeker.[128]

Many critics of private sperm donation state that it should be regulated because donors may have bad intentions. However, this risk is not singular to private donation: it has been well documented in institutionalized donation as well. Between 1976 and 1986, Dr. Cecil Jacobson ("The Sperminator") used his own sperm to "impregnate up to seventy-five of his patients."[129] Worse, he needlessly "treated" patients with "useless drug injections, and he performed needless ... uterus scrapings, on patients who mistakenly believed they were pregnant."[130] Because the risk of abuse is found in every kind of donation, private donation should not suffer. In fact, in private donation, women meet donors and screen them for such egocentric intentions themselves.

D. *Risk of Consanguinity in Institutionalized and Private Donation*

Another risk common to all kinds of donation is consanguinity. There is a potential for accidental consanguinity among children of sperm donors, because of such factors as large numbers of offspring produced by single donors, and donor anonymity.[131]

In September of 2011, the *New York Times* published an article about single sperm donors who have fathered hundred(s) of children through sperm banks.[132] The *ABA Journal* ran a similar article about an attorney whose donations resulted in the birth of at least seventy-five children.[133] *Time Magazine* reports that one British donor has over 1,000 children.[134] Even in states like Texas, which do not have sperm banks, siblings are born to different families in

---

[127] Dokoupil, *supra* note 1.

[128] *Id.*

[129] Alexander N. Hecht, *The Wild Wild West: Inadequate Regulation of Assisted Reproductive Technology*, 1 Hous. J. Health L. & Pol'y 227, 242 (2001).

[130] *Id.* ("In early 1992, Jacobson was convicted on thirty-three felony counts of mail fraud, ten counts of wire fraud, four counts of travel fraud, and six counts of perjury.") (internal citations omitted).

[131] Brzyski, *supra* note 113.

[132] Jacqueline Mroz, *One Sperm Donor, 150 Offspring*, N.Y. Times (Sep. 5, 2011), http://www.nytimes.com/2011/09/06/health/06donor.html?pagewanted-=all.

[133] Debra Cassens Weiss, *Lawyer Learns He Has at Least 75 Children*, A.B.A.J., Sep. 27, 2011, http://www.abajournal.com/news/article/lawyer_learns_he_has_at_least_75_children/.

[134] Newton-Small, *supra* note 40, at 51.

the same metropolitan areas through sperm imported from outside the state.[135]

The possibility of consanguinity is not the only danger that arises from one donor providing sperm to many mothers; an increase in otherwise rare genetic diseases may result from over-donation. Although this article has already discussed the risks of passing on genetic diseases through various sperm donation practices, the possibility of consanguinity between offspring with genetic diseases warrants another look. Ricki Lewis, author of *The Forever Fix: Gene Therapy and the Boy Who Saved It*, argues that without limits on the number of offspring a man may have through sperm donation, there is a higher risk of passing on recessive diseases due to the increased chances of consanguinity.[136] The grandchildren of the sperm donor may be at a higher risk than his children. This is due to the fact that as time passes and the biological children of the donor procreate and their children procreate, there will be more people carrying a dangerous recessive gene. Because there are more carriers, there is a higher likelihood that consanguinity will result in the birth of a child with two sets of recessive genes, a child who has the genetic disease.[137] Eventually, this would lead to the disease becoming more common.

One commonly proposed solution is a system for disclosing sperm donor information and creating limits on the numbers of offspring each donor may have. Currently, the United States does not limit the number of offspring a donor may produce, despite advocacy in favor of such a policy from the American Society for Reproductive Medicine.[138] Wendy Kramer, the creator of the Donor Sibling Registry, which also connects donors with their children,

---

[135] Kimberley King, *Some Call for Regulation of Sperm Banks*, NBC DFW (Oct. 26, 2011), http://www.nbcdfw.com/news/health/Some-Call-for-Regulation-of-Sperm-Banks-132567433.html.

[136] Anneli Rufus, *Are Sperm Banks Unethical?*, ALTERNET (Oct. 13, 2011), www.salon.com/2011/10/13/sperm_bank_ethics/ ("A recessive disease is one that requires both parents to be carriers: Each parent has the mutation, but also a functioning copy of the gene in question too, so he or she is not sick. For a rare disease—say, one that affects one in 10,000 people, or even rarer—the chance of two people being carriers is very low. But if two people are half-siblings, and the sperm donor is a carrier of a recessive disease—and we probably all are—then each partner has a one-half chance of inheriting the mutation... [t]wo unwitting half-sibs bearing a child with a recessive disease such as cystic fibrosis or Tay-Sachs "would be the short-term risk. Longer term, more people in the population would be carriers and, over time, certain inherited diseases would become more common.'").

[137] *Id.*

[138] *Id.*; *see also* Newton-Small, *supra* note 40, at 51.

argues for more regulation when she claims, "we don't know how many kids are born for any one donor, who they are, where they are, if they have any sicknesses, any genetic illnesses ... [t]here's no way to upload and share medical information amongst people who have used the same donor."[139]

Sperm-seekers and donors may prevent their offspring from engaging in accidental consanguinity by continuing to communicate after donation has occurred. Websites such as DonorSiblingRegistry.com may help to prevent consanguinity as well. The website allows donors, donor-conceived children, and the parents of donor-conceived children to sign up using the identifiers that sperm banks gave them. The donor's number matches his child(ren)'s number. Many fathers have met their children, and over 9,000[140] half-siblings, at least,[141] have met using the registry. However, the registry relies on people signing up to match families, and many sperm donors wish to remain anonymous.

Allowing private donation also prevents consanguinity. One reason that some donors have many children is because sperm-seeker banks often use one sperm emission for numerous separate insemination procedures.[142] Further, institutions rely on the sperm-seekers to report their successful pregnancies. Because it is unlikely that each emission by a private donor would be used to father more than one child, private donation could prevent the creation of abundant children from one sperm donor, thereby helping to reduce cases of accidental incest.

There are sometimes legal limits on the number of children sperm donors may produce, but not on how many children a parent may raise. For example, the Duggar family has nineteen children, which is more than Arsenault, a sperm donor, has.[143] Parents that raise many children may help to reduce consanguinity because consanguinity is unlikely to occur among children that know each other. In private donation, half-siblings could potentially know each other as well.[144] For this reason, private donation is safer than

---

[139] *Id.*

[140] DONOR SIBLING REGISTRY, www.donorsiblingregistry.com (last visited Oct. 16, 2012) (The DSR has connected at least 9574 half-siblings (and/or donors) with each other. The total number of registrants, including donors, parents and donor conceived people, is 38134).

[141] Pi, *supra* note 62.

[142] IDANT LABORATORIES, (http://www.idant.com/SemenBank/FAQ.aspx (last visited Oct. 10, 2012).

[143] JIM BOB & MICHELLE DUGGAR FAMILY, http://duggarfamily.com/content/family (last visited Oct. 10, 2012).

[144] Donor Sibling Registry, *supra* note 140 (As mentioned above, the

most institutionalized donation practices, and should remain an option for women.

VI. Paternity Issues in Institutionalized and Private Sperm Donation

A. *Current Laws*

Many sperm donors choose to use institutions to shield themselves from legal parental responsibilities. Fifteen states have statutes stating that sperm donors are not considered "fathers" to their children if the sperm is "provided to a licensed physician for use in artificial insemination of a married woman, other than the donor's wife."[145] It is unclear whether these statutes would also protect private donors.

Other states' laws are more favorable to the donor. These states do not require the sperm to be given to a physician to shield the donor from paternal obligations, and they also prevent a donor from asserting paternal rights against mothers of children conceived through the use of donated sperm.[146] However, these states still require that sperm be given to a married woman, and that her husband's consent must be obtained.[147] This raises another issue:

Donor Sibling Registry may also help those who have already used sperm banking find each other and prevent consanguinity).

[145] Naomi Cahn, *The New Kinship*, 100 Geo. L.J. 367, 387 (2012).

[146] *Id.*

[147] Cal. Fam. Code § 7613 (West 2012). ("(a) If, under the supervision of a licensed physician and surgeon and with the consent of her husband, a wife is inseminated artificially with semen donated by a man not her husband, the husband is treated in law as if he were the natural father of a child thereby conceived. The husband's consent must be in writing and signed by him and his wife. The physician and surgeon shall certify their signatures and the date of the insemination, and retain the husband's consent as part of the medical record, where it shall be kept confidential and in a sealed file. However, the physician and surgeon's failure to do so does not affect the father and child relationship. All papers and records pertaining to the insemination, whether part of the permanent record of a court or of a file held by the supervising physician and surgeon or elsewhere, are subject to inspection only upon an order of the court for good cause shown. (b) The donor of semen provided to a licensed physician and surgeon or to a licensed sperm bank for use in artificial insemination or in vitro fertilization of a woman other than the donor's wife is treated in law as if he were not the natural father of a child thereby conceived, unless otherwise agreed to in a writing signed by the donor and the woman prior to the conception of the child."); *see also* Ala. Code § 26-17-702 (2009) ("A donor who donates to a licensed physician for use by a married woman is not a parent of a child conceived by means of assisted reproduction. A married couple who,

lesbian couples and single women are less likely to obtain sperm in these states because they will not be protected from donors suing to obtain paternity rights.[148] Some argue that these laws "limit the possibility of social change by controlling the medical advances that may enable such a change."[149] Both sets of laws aim to erase any conflicts over paternity between a donor and a married heterosexual couple. However, the laws are outdated: many of the women seeking donor sperm are single women or lesbian couples.

The Uniform Parentage Act prevents donors who provide sperm to single women and lesbian couples from having any paternal rights; the child(ren) will not have a legally recognized father.[150] However, the UPA has not been widely adopted. Sperm donors in some states are not liable for support unless they sign agreements with mothers attesting that they will support the child(ren).[151]

In the Pennsylvania case *Ferguson v. McKiernan*, litigants addressed contracting out of parental rights in sperm donation.[152] The issue was whether a sperm-seeker and sperm donor could "'enter into an enforceable agreement under which the [known] donor provides sperm in a clinical setting for IVF and relinquishes his right to visitation with the resultant child(ren) in return for the mother's agreement not to seek child support from the donor.'"[153]

In a hypothetical situation like the one Beth Gardner proposed, in which two people have a brief sexual encounter resulting in the birth of a child, both parties must provide child support. In

---

under the supervision of a licensed physician, engage in assisted reproduction through use of donated eggs, sperm, or both, will be treated at law as if they are the sole natural and legal parents of a child conceived thereby."). The Alabama Code was "redrafted to continue the prior Alabama practice of protecting a donor from parental responsibilities in only limited situations. *See*, former ALA. CODE § 26-17-21 (1975). This eliminates the potential created in the Uniform Parentage Act of having a child intentionally created who would have no legal father." *Id.*, Editor's Note.

[148] This is just one of many examples of how single women and lesbians do not have the same access to sperm as heterosexual, married women.

[149] Peterson, *supra* note 36 (citing Stuhmcke, *supra* note 39; Anita Stuhmcke, *Limiting Access to Assisted Reproduction: JM v. QFG*, 16 AUSTRL. J. FAM. L. 245 (2002)).

[150] UNIF. PARENTAGE ACT § 5 (1973).

[151] N.H. REV. STAT. ANN. § 168-B:11 (1991) ("A sperm donor may be liable for support only if he signs an agreement with the other parties to that effect."); *see also* CONN. GEN. STAT. ANN. § 45a-775 (West 2007) (An identified or anonymous donor of sperm or eggs used in A.I.D., or any person claiming by or through such donor, shall not have any right or interest in any child born as a result of A.I.D.).

[152] Ferguson v. McKiernan, 940 A.2d 1236, 1241 (2007)·

[153] *Id.*

cases like this, the parties cannot contract out of providing child support. This differs from the situation in *Ferguson,* where a sperm donor and sperm-seeker utilize a sperm bank for the purposes of creating a child and making money. In this case, the Court held that sperm donors are not obligated to the resulting offspring, reasoning that the parties intended, and did, form a binding and valid agreement. Further, the parties made the agreement outside of a romantic relationship, "taking sexual intercourse out of the equation" and tried to preserve anonymity for the donor. This lawsuit has implications for private donations as well, where all of the same contractual elements could be met.

The *Ferguson* court tried to protect women from being forced to choose anonymous donors. If the parties did *not* have a right to contract out of paternity, the court reasoned, donors would be discouraged from providing sperm, and women would not want to risk donor paternity lawsuits. A woman would be unable to assure the sperm donor that he would "never be subject to a support order" and he would not provide her with the assurance that he would "never … seek custody of the child."[154] The court held that distinguishing between sperm donation and brief sexual encounters would leave a woman with no other choice than to seek anonymous donations or to "abandon her desire to be a biological mother."[155] The court noted ""[t]here is simply no basis in law or policy to impose such an unpleasant choice, and to do so would be to legislate in precisely the way … this [c]ourt has no business doing."[156]

Much of the *Ferguson* court's language supported a woman's right to choose her children's father. It stated that some women have a "personal preference to conceive using the sperm of someone familiar, whose background, traits, and medical history are not shrouded in mystery."[157] The court understood that a woman should have the option of choosing a non-anonymous donor, and that the ability to contract out of paternity preserves this option.

Critics may argue that the *Ferguson* ruling impairs the rights of donor-conceived children to get support from or to meet their biological fathers, and therefore the ruling would not be in the children's best interests. Although the children in *Ferguson* would not receive support from the donor, the court reasoned that "[a]bsent the parties' agreement, however, the twins would not have been born at all, or would have been born to a different and anonymous

---

[154] *Id.* at 1246.

[155] *Id.* at 1247.

[156] *Id.* at 1247-48.

[157] *Id.*

sperm donor, who neither party disputes would be safe from a support order."[158]

Though the *Ferguson* case involved a sperm bank, the court's reasoning applies to private donation as well. Although the court's ruling weighed heavily in favor a woman's right to choose her method conception, it still overlooked the benefits of private donation as an alternative to using a sperm bank, as well as the financial burdens and risks of genetic mistakes that can potentially arise from using a sperm bank.

B. *The FDA Should not Regulate Private Donation*

The FDA has recently threatened to fine and imprison Trent Arsenault, a private sperm donor, for refusing to follow the FDA's guidelines for sperm manufacturers.[159] Proponents of more regulation of private sperm donation hailed the decision. However, regulation of private sperm donors would create a large financial cost for the FDA, an organization with already limited resources.[160] Arsenault was the first private donor threatened with fines and imprisonment[161] for "manufacturing" sperm, but what if all private donors were? There are over 6,000 members belonging to the Known Donor Registry, a service that helps private gamete donors meet potential sperm-seekers.[162] It is unlikely that the FDA has the administrative or financial resources to regulate all private donors.

If the FDA were to regulate private donation of sperm, it is unclear how far reaching such regulation would become. The regulations may eventually extend to fining women who seek donated sperm, and other invasions of the private right to conceive free from governmental interference. Some scholars have suggested that the FDA may not be the appropriate regulator of private donation. Ann Althouse, Professor of Law at the University of Wisconsin[163] claims that the FDA has the power to regulate private sperm donation under the Commerce Clause. She equates sperm banks to

---

[158] *Id.* at 1248.

[159] Dokoupil, *supra* note 1.

[160] Heled, *supra* note 118, at 270-72.

[161] Ann Althouse, *Trent Arsenault—Devoted Sperm Donor, Virgin Father —Hounded by the FDA,* ALTHOUSE (Feb. 7, 2012), http://althouse.blogspot.com/2012/02/trent-arsenault-devoted-sperm-donor.html.

[162] Known Donor Registry,*supra* note 6.

[163] Ann Althouse, *About Ann Althouse,* ALTHOUSE, http://althouse.blogspot.com/p/about-ann-althouse.html (last visited Oct. 10, 2012).

marijuana growing operations, stating that the federal government can similarly regulate sperm activity:

> [b]ecause it regulates the sperm bank business and this is like the way it can regulate growing one marijuana plant even one that isn't intended for the commercial market? But marijuana is a commodity, and—as the Supreme Court said in Gonzales v. Raich—"the regulation is squarely within Congress' commerce power because production of the commodity meant for home consumption, be it wheat or marijuana, has a substantial effect on supply and demand in the national market for that commodity.

Professor Althouse argues that the FDA can regulate private donation because the sale of sperm by sperm banks is lucrative, and private donation, in the aggregate, can interfere with sperm bank profits. However, sperm is not the same as marijuana or other commodities covered under the Commerce Clause; each specimen is a natural function of the human body, made by a living and breathing person, and used to create another life. Creating a child is a personal and intimate act, as Arsenault has argued, and sperm donation is a private sexual matter, and therefore the federal government should not regulate private donation.[164] Production of sperm is an inherent characteristic and an intrinsic part of being a male human, and unlike marijuana, which is strictly a commodity. For these reasons, the FDA should not be allowed to regulate private sperm donation under the Commerce Clause.

C. *Current Guidelines for Institutions that are Useful to Private Sperm-seekers*

The American Society of Reproductive Medicine (ASRM) and the American Association of Tissue Banks (AATB) have created non-mandatory[165] guidelines explaining how to prevent the spread of genetic and sexually transmitted diseases in sperm donation transactions.[166] The sanction for noncompliance of a sperm bank with the AATB Guidelines is withdrawal of accreditation

---

[164] Dokoupil, *supra* note 1. *See also* Lawrence v. Texas, 539 U.S. 558, 578 (2003); Cruzan v. Mo. Dep't. of Health, 497 U.S. 261 (1990); Roe v. Wade, 410 U.S. 113 (1973), *modified by* Planned Parenthood of Se. Pa. v. Casey, 505 U.S. 833 (1992); Griswold v Connecticut, 381 U.S. 479 (1965).

[165] Heled, *supra* note 118, at 270-72.

[166] *Id.*

"'upon a determination ... that significant non-compliance, such as repeated violations, one or more egregious violations, uncorrected violations or deliberate falsehoods, have occurred.'"[167] The regulation is very loose, and many aspects of donation that it seeks to regulate, such as STD's, genetic diseases, and fertility, are all things that many private donors, such as Arsenault, regularly make public. However, women seeking private sperm donations might use such guidelines to help determine if particular donors are safe.

Legislators and agencies such as the FDA are usually reluctant to regulate human reproductive issues.[168] The CDC, FDA, and many states agencies currently do not even regulate testing for genetic diseases in gametes, focusing instead on the potential for spreading STD's and STI's.[169] New York and Ohio are the only states that require genetic testing for diseases.[170] New York requires tissue banks to meet such qualifications, but not private donors.[171] However, private parties may self-monitor through relatively inexpensive tests. The statute, as a public document, may even act as a guideline to private parties, lessening the need for regulation. Ohio has laws that cover when and how sperm may be used for "non -spousal artificial insemination."[172] The laws require that certain healthcare professionals follow the statutes, but do not state that private parties must meet the requirements. Many of the requirements are similar to those provided in the AATB guidelines.[173] New

---

[167] *Id.* (internal citation omitted).

[168] *Id.* at 248.

[169] *Id.* at 255.

[170] *Id.* at 250-58.

[171] N.Y. COMP. CODES R. & REGS. TIT. 10, § 52-8.5 (1991).

[172] OHIO REV. CODE ANN. § 3111.91 (West 2000).

[173] *Id.* ("(A) In a non-spousal artificial insemination, fresh or frozen semen may be used, provided that the requirements of division (B) of this section are satisfied.

(B)(1) A physician, physician assistant, clinical nurse specialist, certified nurse practitioner, certified nurse-midwife, or person under the supervision and control of a physician may use fresh semen for purposes of a non-spousal artificial insemination, only if within one year prior to the supplying of the semen, all of the following occurred:

(a) A complete medical history of the donor, including, but not limited to, any available genetic history of the donor, was obtained by a physician, a physician assistant, a clinical nurse specialist, or a certified nurse practitioner.

(b) The donor had a physical examination by a physician, a physician assistant, a clinical nurse specialist, or a certified nurse practitioner.

(c) The donor was tested for blood type and RH factor.

Hampshire requires that sperm donors must be medically evaluated before making a donation.[174] The statute seems to cover all artificial insemination, whether done through an institution or in a Starbucks bathroom. It is also arguably overbroad, in that it could apply to every sexual act that could inseminate a woman.

These laws mostly apply to sperm banks, and not to private donors. Similar to the way a person might look at the nutritional guidelines before eating at a fast food restaurant, a private sperm-seeker could look to these laws as guidelines on how to find a donor, become pregnant, and retain custody of her child. Simply because a product has the potential to be detrimental to health does not mean that it must be regulated. If we have the choice to eat Big Macs, french fries and to drink soda despite knowing that they are always unhealthy, then women should have the option to assume the risk of private sperm donation, especially because every sample of sperm does not carry STI's or genetic diseases.

D. *Lawsuits are a Potential Avenue for "Regulation"*

In some states, a donee may file a lawsuit against a donor or sperm bank under the wrongful life theory. California, Washington, and New Jersey allow claimants to bring wrongful life actions for

---

(2) A physician, physician assistant, clinical nurse specialist, certified nurse practitioner, certified nurse-midwife, or person under the supervision and control of a physician may use frozen semen for purposes of a non-spousal artificial insemination only if all the following apply:
(a) The requirements set forth in division (B)(1) of this section are satisfied;
(b) In conjunction with the supplying of the semen, the semen or blood of the donor was the subject of laboratory studies that the physician involved in the non-spousal artificial insemination considers appropriate. The laboratory studies may include, but are not limited to, venereal disease research laboratories, karotyping, GC culture, cytomegalo, hepatitis, kem-zyme, Tay-Sachs, sickle-cell, ureaplasma, HLTV-III, and chlamydia.
(c) The physician involved in the non-spousal artificial insemination determines that the results of the laboratory studies are acceptable results.
(3) Any written documentation of a physical examination conducted pursuant to division (B)(1)(b) of this section shall be completed by the individual who conducted the examination.").

[174] N.H. REV. STAT. ANN. § 168-B:10 (2011) ("No semen shall be used in an insemination procedure unless the sperm donor has been medically evaluated and the results, documented in accordance with any rules adopted by the department of health and human services, demonstrate the medical acceptability of the person as a sperm donor.").

recovery of damages for medical treatment and therapy.[175] Most other jurisdictions do not allow wrongful life actions even when a donor-conceived child in question suffers from a genetically inherited impairment.[176] Courts that do not recognize wrongful life actions because "general damages in such cases are impossible to measure, since the damages to be calculated would be the difference between the child's life with defects or disease, and the utter void of nonexistence."[177] Cases brought under a wrongful life theory have not been successful. However, in states that do not recognize wrongful life actions, wrongful death cases have been brought successfully when a mother or her child has passed away due to an STI or STD such as HIV contracted through infected sperm provided to her from a cryobank.[178]

In *Johnson v. Superior Court of Los Angeles County*, a cryobank in California knew that the donor had a genetic disorder and still accepted him as a donor, but did not inform the sperm-seeker of the defect.[179] The bank stated that it had screened the sperm. Because of this misstatement, a child was born with the disorder that the sperm donor carried.[180] The complaint stated that the donor could have fathered as many as 1,600 children through the sperm bank.[181] A private donor is unlikely to sire so many children because usually in private donations, one sample will be used to produce only one child, in contrast with institutionalized donations, where one sample is used many times. If the mother in *Johnson* had chosen a private sperm donor, her child may not have inherited a genetic disease. She would not have relied on a cryobank, and would have been able to screen donors herself for genetic disease. Even if the sperm-seeker had chosen the genetically "deficient" sperm, then she would be less likely to use limited judicial resources, because, as the primary decision making party, she would not have grounds to sue, unless the donor had concealed

---

[175] 50 AM. JUR. 2D *Trials* § 1 (1994).

[176] *Id.*

[177] Heled, *supra* note 118, at 262-63.

[178] *Id.* ("Where negligence of the sperm bank consisting of unreasonable donor HIV screening practices results in the transmission of AIDS to the recipient wife or her child causing death, an action for wrongful death brought against the sperm bank is an appropriate remedy. A wrongful death action would permit the survivors of the AIDS victim to recover for losses occasioned by the sperm bank's negligence. As a rule, wrongful death actions sound in negligence and involve the same elements as negligence actions.") (internal citation omitted).

[179] *Id.* at 270-72.

[180] *Id.*

[181] *Id.*, at 264.

information from her. In such a case, it might be more difficult for a mother to sue a sperm bank than a private donor for defective material because donor records kept by sperm banks are secret and confidential. This may not be an issue in private donation, because the sperm-seeker has the option of requiring donor genetic tests and disclosure of medical records.

VII. CONCLUSION

Private sperm donation is becoming more prevalent for multiple reasons. It is less financially burdensome to potential recipients than institutionalized donation, information about all types of sperm donation is more readily and easily accessible to donees, and many men prefer private donation. Lesbian couples and single women use private donation because they lack equitable access to institutionalized sperm donation. Further, the media has recently increased the visibility of private donation. Finally, fresh sperm is more likely to result in pregnancy than the frozen sperm which sperm bank institutions are required to use.

Despite, or perhaps because of, the increasing prevalence of private sperm donation, the FDA recently cracked down on Trent Arsenault, a private sperm donor, ordering him to "cease manufacture" of sperm. This poses a critical question: should private donation be regulated like institutionalized sperm donation, or should women have the right to choose between unregulated private, and regulated institutionalized, donation?

There are several reasons why private donation should not be regulated. Women have more power over whether their children learn the identity of their biological father, and the sperm donor can choose to identify himself. Both participants can decide whether the sperm donor should have access to the child, or whether he should pay child support.

In response to the outcry against some of the problems that come through institutionalized procreation, many call for the creation of a national registry of sperm donors. They argue that this would prevent the spread of genetic or sexually transmitted diseases, and would limit the number of children one donor could create. Even if a national registry would help solve some of these problems, it would be nearly impossible to create and enforce, and would likely trigger a decrease in sperm donations.

There are risks and benefits associated with both institutionalized and private donation. Potential problems include the spread of genetic or sexually transmitted diseases, and conflicts over paternity. These risks are often shared with institutionalized donation. Some of the risks associated solely with institutionalized donation include confusion of sperm samples in the insemination process, accidental disposal of tissue, improper maintenance of samples, and the increased potential for consanguinity. Because private donation reduces or eliminates these issues, it should remain an option for women.

The FDA should not regulate private donation. However, the guidelines promulgated by the FDA and other institutions can be used by private sperm-seekers to screen potential sperm donors. When a private sperm transaction goes awry, a lawsuit should be the appropriate method to resolve the issue. None of the risks of private donation warrant an intrusion into a woman's right to choose between private and institutionalized donation. Many of the women choose private donation because they are unable to access sperm banks, due to gender and sexual orientation discrimination, and/or the high financial cost of institutionalized donation. Some women want to have more power to choose a sperm donor and to decide how her children will interact with him. Others do not trust sperm banks to perform the requisite tests and to use the correct sperm in the insemination procedure. The FDA should not force these women to bend to its will. Sperm-seekers should be allowed to choose their sperm donor and method of insemination. After all, "[i]f it's legal to go to a bar, get drunk, and sleep with a random stranger, then it can't possibly be illegal to provide clean, healthy sperm in a cup."[182]

---

[182] Dokoupil, *supra* note 1 (quoting Beth Gardner).

"CAN YOU HEAR ME NOW...GOOD!"[®1] FEMINISM(S), THE PUBLIC/PRIVATE DIVIDE, AND *CITIZENS UNITED V. FEC*[2]

Ronnie Cohen* and Shannon O'Byrne**

I. INTRODUCTION

An important goal identified by early feminists was to challenge and even eliminate the distinction between the public and private spheres. Though by no means uniformly, these feminists rejected the liberal notion—broadly stated—that the public sphere (including governmental power) should not impinge on the private realm where "individuals are the final arbiters of their decisions."[3] The private sphere—idealized by the notions of hearth and home—denigrated and endangered women in part by isolating them and rendering them subject to male control, including by way of domestic violence. According to Raia Prokhovnik, feminist critiques regarded the public/private divide as "the source of women's oppression, not only because the private realm is exempt from liberal principles and political accountability, but also because activity and work in the private realm are not valued like that in civil society."[4]

---

* Professor, Luter School of Business, Christopher Newport University, Newport News, VA (rcohen@cnu.edu)

** Professor, Faculty of Law, University of Alberta, Edmonton, Alberta, Canada (sobyrne@ualberta.ca)

[1] "Can You Hear Me Now? Good." Registration No. 2,829,096.

[2] Citizens United v. Fed. Election Comm'n, 558 U.S. 310 (2010).

[3] Raia Prokhovnik, *Public and Private Citizenship: From Gender Invisibility to Feminist Inclusiveness*, 60 FEMINIST REV. 84, 87 (Autumn 1998).

[4] *Id.*

Under the slogan that "the personal is the political,"[5] certain feminists called for the end to a sharply defined public/private distinction with the goal of ending the contemptuous, brutal treatment of women by men. As Carole Pateman famously declared in 1983, "[t]he dichotomy between the private and the public is central to almost two centuries of feminist writing and political struggle; it is, ultimately, what the feminist movement is about."[66]

Indeed, feminists have shown over time and discipline exactly what the public/private distinction has meant for women. Sociologically, the divide has reflected and brought violence against them in the home and beyond. It has meant the devaluation of their domestic work. And it has objectified and repressed their sexuality. Politically, the distinction has stifled women's voices in public discourse. Legally, it has legitimized discriminatory practices against them in their homes and in the marketplace—the latter an arena closely aligned with the anti-state perspective of the private sphere.

In response, prominent strands of feminism(s) attacked the public/private distinction in order to institute and advance women's physical, psychological, political and economic safety and well being. But as feminists sought to challenge the public/private distinction by making the private more public, corporations (representing the hierarchical, male-dominated private sector that feminists were opposing) were also resisting the divide between public and private, but with a pernicious intent. Through lobbying, campaign contributions, sheer economic power, and most recently, by a largely unsolicited boost from the United States Supreme Court in *Citizens United v. FEC,* corporations have worked to privatize much of the public sphere—up to and including the electoral process in the United States. In short, while feminists rallied around the notion that the private is the public, large corporate interests were quietly insisting that the public is the private.

A central purpose of this essay is to critique *Citizens United,* and to explore how feminism(s) might respond to the decision and

---

   [5] The origin of the phrase "the personal is the political" has been traced to Carol Hanisch's 1969 paper *The Personal is Political.* Hanisch confirms that she used the word "political" broadly, to refer to "power relationships, not [just] the narrow sense of electorial [sic] politics." Carol Hanisch, Introduction, *The Personal Is Political,* 1 (Jan. 2006), http://www.carolhanisch.org/CHwritings/PersonalisPol.pdf (including both original article and 2006 Introduction; original article was first published in Carole Hanisch, *The Personal Is Political, in* Notes From the Second Year: Women's Liberation 76 (Shulamith Firestone ed., 1970)).
   [6] Carole Pateman, *Feminist Critiques of the Public/Private Dichotomy, in* Public and Private in Social Life 281, 281 (S.I. Benn & G.F. Gaus eds., 1983).

its privatization of the public electoral process. In *Citizens United*, a 5:4 majority of the U.S. Supreme Court ruled that restrictions on direct expenditures from corporate treasuries to support or oppose candidates for political office were unconstitutional restrictions on corporations' rights to free speech. According to the majority opinion, monetary contributions are a form of protected speech under the First Amendment, and that a corporation, and not a natural person, made the speech at issue was found to have no significance.[7] In so ruling, the Court equated corporations with citizens and gave them exactly equivalent constitutional protection in relation to political expression.

We propose a two-pronged feminist attack against *Citizens United*. First, we advance the feminist strategy of recalibrating theory in light of what is happening 'on the ground', thereby identifying dangers facing women which emerge under new or modified guises—in this case, the privatization of the electoral process.[8] To reveal the unsound foundations of *Citizens United*, we perceive an urgent need for aspects of feminism(s) to defend as distinct a robustly construed public domain.[9] This will help to halt the usurpation of the public interest by private economic power. Second, we deploy feminism(s) well-known rejection of abstraction in favor of context. This too will castigate *Citizens United*'s strategic refusal to make distinctions even when they are obvious and context would call for nothing less. As this essay will show, *Citizens United* propels its outcome by erasing tremendously significant legal distinctions—most crucially between living human beings and artificial legal entities. Upon putting in place the boldly and patently false premise that corporations and natural persons are overwhelmingly analogous, the Court goes on to deny the distinction between the

---

[7] *See Citizens United*, 558 U.S. at 339-341.

[8] See Mike McIntire & Nicholas Confessore, *Tax-Exempt Groups Shield Political Gifts of Businesses*, N.Y.TIMES, July 7, 2012, http://www.nytimes.com/2012/07/08/us/politics/groups-shield-political-gifts-of-businesses.html?_r=1&nl=todaysheadlines&emc=edit_th_20120708, for a discussion of how much corporate spending in the political arena has ramped up in light of *Citizens United*. In the elections since 2010, though for- profit corporations are not the largest donors to candidates or Super-Pacs, they are significant donors to non-profit corporations that advocate for issues closely aligned with candidates' positions.

[9] The problem of a diminishing public space is widespread. As Janine Brodie notes, this "reprivatiz[ation]" of what was once public "create[s] new norms and expectations about what is 'up for grabs' in politics and, ultimately about the role of the citizen." Janine Brodie, *Shifting the Boundaries: Gender and the Politics of Restructuring, in* THE STRATEGIC SILENCE: GENDER AND ECONOMIC POLICY 46, 56 (Isabella Bakker ed. 1994).

public sphere populated by citizens and the private sphere populated by corporate profit takers; between political self-expression and corporate spending; between individual suffrage and business transactions. By erasing distinctions, the Supreme Court elevated the private to an absurd and destructive level. This is because large and monied economic interests—many of which are advantaged by limited liability and large aggregations of capital—become the "loudest voice in town."[10] Such dominance comes at the obvious and lamentable expense of ordinary human persons, and is exacerbated for women and other disadvantaged groups.

The following essay is divided into several parts. Part II provides a brief account of feminist perspectives on the public/private distinction. Though an important early challenge for feminism(s) was to break down the barriers between public and private (because such distinctions isolated women in the private sphere and effected their subjugation), destruction of barriers can also exacerbate disadvantage depending on who is in charge of the exercise. In short, as this part illustrates, increasing privatization of the public sphere creates new vulnerabilities. With this context in place, Part III analyses the *Citizens United* case. It shows that the majority, by *completely* erasing the distinction between citizens and corporations, between the public and the private, has very much reduced the power of human beings to participate in the public sphere. This part also relies on the insights of feminism(s) to criticize the majority for strategically and wrongfully advancing abstraction over context. Part IV suggests some possible correctives to the Supreme Court majority's analysis, based on the insights of feminism(s) and progressive corporate law scholars. The essay concludes by calling for an enhanced feminist presence in defining the public realm and repelling a hostile corporate takeover of public space.

Feminists have historically fought against male power on a variety of fronts, but with few exceptions,[11] have been less inclined

---

[10] William Patton & Randall Bartlett, *Corporate "Persons" and Freedom of Speech: The Political Impact of Legal Mythology*, 1981 Wis. L. Rev. 494, 502 (1981).

[11] A representative sampling of the work of these authors includes: Ronnie Cohen, *Feminist Thought and Corporate Law: It's Time to Find Our Way Up From the Bottom (Line)*, 2 Am. U. J. Gender & L. 1 (1994); Mary Condon, *Gendering the Pension Promise in Canada: Risk, Financial Markets and Neoliberalism*, 10 Soc. and Legal Stud. 83 (2001); Lynne L. Dallas, *Short-Termism, the Financial Crisis, and Corporate Governance*, 37 J. Corp. L. 265 (2012); Theresa A. Gabaldon, *The Lemonade Stand: Feminist and Other Reflections on the Limited Liability of Corporate Shareholders*, 45 Vand. L. Rev. 1387 (1992); Kathleen A. Lahey & Sara W. Salter, *Corporate Law in Legal Theory and Legal Scholarship:*

to tackle issues of corporate structure and governance. This has left a treacherous lacuna. The outcome in *Citizens United* shows that a broader feminist strategy is required; one which increases its presence in corporate law critiques. Such a presence will help halt—or at least identify and decry—the advance of corporations at the expense of real citizens.

II. THE PUBLIC-PRIVATE DISTINCTION

What the public-private distinction means in context diverges widely within and between disciplines.[12] Feminist traditions are no different and it is certainly beyond the scope of this essay to offer a thorough accounting of scholarship in the area. We do, however, observe that the dichotomy itself has ancient roots in Western thought as a "binary opposition that is used to subsume a wide range of other important distinctions and that attempts...to dichotomize the social universe in a comprehensive and sharply demarcated way."[13] As Joan Landes notes:

> Feminists did not invent the vocabulary of public and private, which in ordinary language and political tradition have been intimately linked. The term 'public' suggests the opposite of 'private': that which pertains to the people as a whole, the community, the common good, things open to sight, and those things that are accessible and shared by all. Conversely, 'the private' signifies something closed and exclusive, as in the admonition 'Private property—no trespassing.'[14]

From a legal standpoint, privacy manifests itself as a boundary which the law (and its agents) cannot cross absent special circumstances. The contexts in which this boundary exists are numerous:

From Classicism to Feminism, 23 OSGOODE HALL L.J. 543 (1985); Janis Sarra, *The Gender Implications of Corporate Governance Change*, 1 SEATTLE J. FOR SOC. JUST. 457 (2002); Kellye Y. Testy, *Capitalism and Freedom—For Whom? Feminist Legal Theory and Progressive Corporate Law*, 67 LAW & CONTEMP. PROBS. 87 (Autumn 2004).

[12] *See* Jeff Weintraub, *The Theory and Politics of the Public/Private Distinction, in* PUBLIC AND PRIVATE IN THOUGHT AND PRACTICE: PERSPECTIVES ON A GRAND DICHOTOMY 1, 7-34 (Jeff Weintraub & Krishan Kumar eds.,1997) (discussing four major ways in which the public-private distinction is approached but not claiming the list to be exhaustive).

[13] *Id.* at 1.

[14] Joan B. Landes, Introduction, *in* FEMINISM, THE PUBLIC AND THE PRIVATE 1, 1-2 (Joan B. Landes ed., 1998).

family law where judges have historically been reluctant to interfere with the relationships among family members,[15] personal reproductive decisions where courts have carved out a zone of privacy into which the government's authority may not enter,[16] and personal spaces which are not subject to government search absent a warrant or other public necessity.[17]

The public/private distinction also creates a boundary between government and the private sector of business, capital and markets. In this latter configuration, the reach of government, through law and regulation, is limited in its ability to affect transactions. Similarly, the judiciary classically takes a 'hands-off' approach to what market participants do by refusing, for example, to evaluate the fairness of a bargain.[18] Frances Olsen characterized these different contexts in which the privacy boundary exists as the market/family dichotomy which separates the public world of work and commerce from the private world of the home, and the state/civil society dichotomy that distinguishes the state from the rest of the society-public, including individuals and nongovernmental

---

[15] *See* Sally F. Goldfarb, *Reconceiving Civil Protection Orders for Domestic Violence: Can Law Help End the Abuse without Ending the Relationship?* 29 CARDOZO L. REV. 1487, 1494 (2008).

[16] *See, e.g.*, Griswold v. Connecticut, 381 U.S 479, 484-85 (1965).

[17] In *Kyllo v. United States*, the Supreme Court reiterated the long-standing principle that the Fourth Amendment draws "a firm line at the entrance to the house," beyond which the government may not enter without a warrant. 533 U.S. 27, 40 (2001) (quotation and citation omitted).

[18] See Jay M. Feinman, *Critical Approaches to Contract Law,* 30 UCLA L. REV. 829, 831-34 (1983) for a discussion of classical contract law's "tendency to regard contract as within the exclusive realm of private ordering."

groups.[19] Darren Rosenblum depicts Olsen's analysis in the following way:[20]

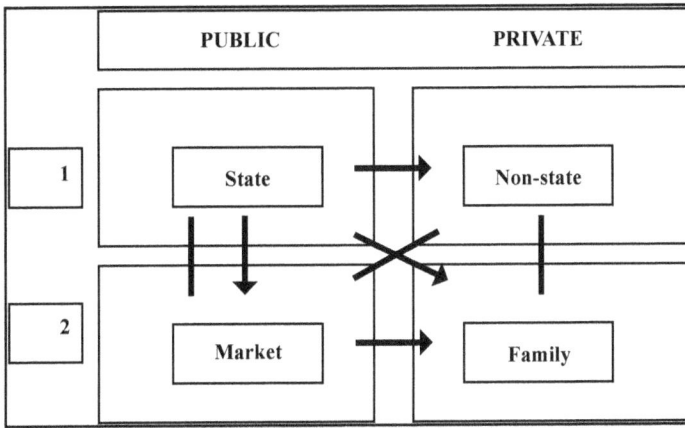

In this model, the market is part of the public sphere while the family is the chief inhabitant of the private sphere. But the market is *also* represented with the family as a non-state entity. This is an important development in illustrating that the market's reach in both the public and private spheres. According to Rosenblum the "use of 'public/private' suggests the dichotomy between state and non-state actors, as well as the market and the family." [21]

Speaking generally, feminist jurisprudence rejected the public/private boundary as an acceptable rationale for legal action or inaction.[22] Feminists argued that in a great many situations, the bound-

---

[19] Frances E. Olsen, *International Law: Feminist Critiques of the Public Private Distinction, in* RECONCEIVING REALITY: WOMEN AND INTERNATIONAL LAW 157, 158 (Dorinda G. Dallmeyer ed., 1993).

[20] Darren Rosenblum, *Feminizing Capital: A Corporate Imperative*, 6 BERKELEY BUS. L.J. 55, 70 (2009).

[21] *Id.* at 69.

[22] This is, in part, why many feminists rejected Hannah Arendt's view of the public/private dichotomy. Arendt believed that our public interests as citizens are quite distinct from our private interests as individuals and that there was a particular space which she called the "space of appearance" where we engage our public interests and shared values. Interestingly, the financial domination of the public space enabled by *Citizens United* would have troubled Arendt, as her view of public space was a place where citizens would interact, exchange ideas, and each citizen would have an effective voice. *See* Maurizio Passerin D'Entrèves, *Public and Private in Hannah Arendt's Conception of Citizenship*, *in* PUBLIC AND PRIVATE: LEGAL, POLITICAL AND PHILOSOPHICAL PERSPECTIVES 68, 69-71 (Maurizio Passerin d'Entrèves and Ursula Vogul eds., 2000) (discussing Hannah Arendt's conception of the "space of appearance").

ary disadvantages women and the institutions with which women are traditionally associated—such as the family—and privileges the group holding the most power in society, namely, white men, and the institutions they control: business organizations. This criticism of the dichotomy applied to both the market/family and the state/civil society constructs. In response to these insights, feminism(s) historically sought to break down the public/private divide in order to enhance scrutiny of the treatment of women. As Weintraub summarizes the matter, feminist challenges to the public/private divide traditionally included at least three overlapping arguments:

> One is that the conceptual orientations of much social and political theory have ignored the domestic sphere or treated it as trivial. The second is that the public/private distinction itself is often deeply gendered, and in almost uniformly invidious ways. It very often plays a role in ideologies that purport to assign men and women to different spheres of social life on the basis of their 'natural' characteristics and thus to confine women to positions of inferiority. The third is that, by classifying institutions like the family as 'private'... the public/private distinctions often serve to shield abuse and domination within these relationships from political scrutiny or legal redress.[23]

Indeed, some feminists—most notably Catherine MacKinnon—called for an end to the separation of public and private.[24] Associating the private realm with oppression, MacKinnon clearly stated: "This is why feminism has had to explode the private. This is why feminism has seen the personal as the political. The private is public for those for whom the personal is political. In this sense, for women there is no private, either normatively or empirically."[25] As Ruth Gavison notes, for this strand of feminism, the aphorism that "the personal is the political" challenged the very existence of two distinct spheres. Within this context, Gavison observes:

> The "personal" should not be allowed to stop conversations, critique, or accountability; the "personal" should not be seen as an improper theme for concern

---

[23] Weintraub, *supra* note 12, at 28-29.

[24] Ruth Gavison, *Feminism and the Public/Private Distinction*, 45 Stan. L. Rev. 1, 1-2 (1992) (noting MacKinnon's challenge to the public/private distinction).

[25] Catharine A. MacKinnon, Toward a Feminist Theory of the State 191 (1989); Gavison, *supra* note 24, at 2 (quoting the same from MacKinnon).

and possible public interference. It is against this background of *this* interpretation of "personal" that the slogan ["the personal is political"] should be understood ...
[For example,] [w]hen women are battered at home, it is
not because each particular victim has triggered an un-
fortunate "individual" tragedy. . . . Social structures are
involved, social structures which are not simply "natural." They are person-made, and they benefit males.[26]

The idea is that the boundary between public and private cannot be
drawn because, as Jean Cohen sums up this strand, such boundaries
work to "exclud[e], denigrat[e], and dominat[e]. . . those designated
as 'different'"[27] from the white, heterosexual male baseline.

But that said, other strands of feminism(s) have insisted on
preserving the public/private dichotomy because the private sphere
"may actually capture a difference that is meaningful to women's
experiences."[28] As Martha Ackelsberg and Mary Lyndon Shanley
observed in 1996 in relation to the public/private divide, feminists
have also understood that women have an interest in privacy rights
relating to a wide array of matters—from custody of their children,
to reproductive freedoms, to choosing a life partner.[29] As another
example in relation to violence against women, Higgins has more
recently argued that recognizing the private sphere as distinct from
the public sphere can be illuminating in terms of understanding
both the harm experienced by women and how that harm should
be addressed at an individual and policy level.[30]

Other critiques illustrate how analysis of the public/private
divide by certain strands of feminism(s) betrays bias—including
that of race and class—which, egregious on its own footing, also

---

[26] Gavison, *supra* note 24, at 19-20.

[27] Jean L. Cohen, *Rethinking Privacy: Autonomy, Identity, and the Abortion Controversy, in* PUBLIC AND PRIVATE IN THOUGHT AND PRACTICE: PERSPECTIVES ON A GRAND DICHOTOMY, *supra* note 12, at 133, 134.

[28] Tracy E. Higgins, *Reviving the Public/Private Distinction in Feminist Theorizing,* 75 CHI.-KENT L. REV. 847, 861 (2000).

[29] Martha A. Ackelsberg & Mary Lyndon Shanley, *Privacy, Publicity, and Power: A Feminist Rethinking of the Public-Private Distinction, in* REVISIONING THE POLITICAL: FEMINIST RECONSTRUCTIONS OF TRADITIONAL CONCEPTS IN WESTERN POLITICAL THEORY 213, 213 (Nancy J. Hirschmann & Christine Di Stefano eds., 1996).

[30] *See* Higgins, *supra* note 28, at 862-66.

stunts analysis. For example, bell hooks points to how the private sphere can be a site of empowerment, stating:

> Historically, African-American people believed that the construction of a homeplace, however fragile and tenuous (the slave hut, the wooden shack), had a radical political dimension. Despite the brutal reality of racial apartheid, of domination, one's homeplace was the one site where one could freely confront the issue of humanization, where one could resist.[31]

In another interpretation, feminists such as Carol Gilligan urge the infusion of private sphere values into the public consciousness. Thus, the "ethic of care" is a means of instilling the "feminine voice" into the predominantly abstract, hierarchical masculine public sphere.[32]

Yet another strand finds utility in maintaining a public/private distinction but with a particular focus on the public sphere. Christine Sypnowich, for example, ardently defends the distinction. She agrees with feminists that the private sphere has, historically, been a sphere of oppression for women and minorities, but asserts that the rule of law is an "institution which helps ensure that we are accorded worth and dignity in the domain of the public, that we are included and counted as citizens. But the rule of law also seeks to leave us unimpeded and unseen in our particular personal domains, according us respect as private persons."[33]

The foregoing selection of feminist analyses of the public/private divide suggests a diverse and productive community. It also suggests that the approaches which feminism(s) takes to the public/private dichotomy—even when opposed—are inherently driven by the context of the problem at hand. For example, when the issue is domestic violence against women and privacy is raised as a

---

[31] bell hooks, YEARNING: RACE, GENDER, AND CULTURAL POLITICS 42 (1990). More generally, feminists have expressed concern that the public/private analysis is exclusionary. As Susan Boyd expresses the matter: "[I]t has been shown that most feminist literature on the public private divide tends to identify gender as the primary cause of women's oppression, thereby diminishing the potential of an analysis that examines the role of race, culture, class, sexuality, and disability..." Susan B. Boyd, *Challenging the Public/Private Divide: An Overview*, in CHALLENGING THE PUBLIC/PRIVATE DIVIDE: FEMINISM, LAW, AND PUBLIC POLICY 3, 12 (Susan B. Boyd ed., 1997).

[32] *See* CAROL GILLIGAN, IN A DIFFERENT VOICE: PSYCHOLOGICAL THEORY AND WOMEN'S DEVELOPMENT 173 (1982).

[33] Christine Sypnowich, *The Civility of Law Between Public and Private*, in PUBLIC AND PRIVATE: LEGAL, POLITICAL AND PHILOSOPHICAL PERSPECTIVES, *supra* note 22, at 93, 113.

block, a feminist response is to deny the legitimacy of the boundary between public and private because it is being used oppressively. And when a women's right to choose a life partner is challenged by homophobism, feminism(s) will raise a woman's right to privacy and private sphere rights to determine for oneself what constitutes family.[34]

Returning to *Citizens United*, part of the context it reflects is that corporate private power has grown dramatically while public power has decreased. For example, over the course of the last century, many public functions have been privatized, from the U.S. war effort in Iraq[35] to the creation of whole communities by private corporations, such as Celebration, Florida.[36] Voucher programs to replace public delivery of services such as education,[37] and proposals to replace Social Security with individual savings accounts[38] and Medicare with private insurance plans[39] are further examples of the trend towards privatization. The public street corner, once the main site for public speech, is being replaced by the privately controlled Internet as the increasingly popular platform for public communication.[40] Indeed, Matthew Diller suggests "[p]rivatization may

---

[34] *See* Acklesberg & Shanley, *supra* note 29, at 225.

[35] T. Christian Miller, *Contractors Outnumber Troops in Iraq; The Figure, Higher Than Reported Earlier, Doesn't Include Security Firms. Critics Say the Issue is Accountability.*, L.A. TIMES, July 4, 2007, http://search.proquest.com/docview/422208625?accountid=14512.

[36] *See Tour of Celebration*, TOWN CENTER, CELEBRATION, FL, http://www.celebrationtowncenter.com/tour-of-celebration-town-center (last visited Oct. 14, 2012) (describing Celebration's development under private companies); *see also* David Segal, *Our Town Inc*, N.Y. TIMES, June 24, 2012, http://search.proquest.com/docview/1021977532?accountid=14512 (describing the privatization of municipal functions in Sandy Springs, Ga.).

[37] *See Education Program: Publicly Funded School Voucher Programs*, NATIONAL CONFERENCE OF STATE LEGISLATURES, http://www.ncsl.org/issues-research/educ/school-choice-vouchers.aspx (last visited Oct. 14, 2012) (describing state school voucher initiatives that use public funding to pay for private education through vouchers).

[38] *See* Social Security Personal Savings Guarantee and Prosperity Act of 2005, H.R. 1776, 109th Cong. (2005).

[39] *See e.g.*, H.R. Con. Res. 34, 112th Cong. (2012) (as reported by H. Comm. on the Budget) (reporting the resolution for adoption of Rep. Paul Ryan's budget proposal); H.R. Rep. No. 112-58, at 103-106 (2012) (accompanying H.R. Con. Res. 34 and describing the proposed privatization of Medicare).

[40] See Ronnie Cohen & Janine S. Hiller, *Towards a Theory of CyberPlace: A Proposal for a New Legal Framework*, 10 RICH. J.L. & TECH. 41 (2003) for a discussion of the movement of speech from the public to the private sphere, and the consequential regulatory shift from the First Amendment to contractual terms of use with internet service providers under a framework of private property rights.

be linked to the growing reality that governments are more at the mercy of markets than the other way around."[41]

In the private sphere, the basic relationship between the provider and the recipient of goods or services is contractual. Private law controls the transaction, and thus, private interests may supersede the interests of the citizens for whom these benefits are obtained by the state. For example, in December 2011, the *New York Times* reported that increasingly, school lunch programs are using private food service companies who work with private food processors to supply school lunches.[42] The allocation of agricultural surplus provided to the schools by the Department of Agriculture is turned over to food processors and then turned into products like chicken nuggets. Driven by the profit motive, the private sector over-processes food destined for children's lunches. The result is an inferior product, characterized by decreased nutritional value. In fact, according to the article, "[a] 2008 study by the Robert Wood Johnson Foundation found that by the time many healthier commodities reach students, 'they have about the same nutritional value as junk foods.'"[43] As the story notes, the school lunch program becomes about profit maximization (a private sphere value) when it should be about health for school children (a public sphere value). We observe that this use of private power (the food processors and

---

[41] Matthew Diller, *Introduction: Redefining the Public Sector: Accountability and Democracy in the Era of Privatization,* 28 FORDHAM URB. L.J. 1307, 1309 (2001) (discussing the manner in which the government carries out its functions). For analysis of prison privatization as another example, see Sharon Dolovich, *State Punishment and Private Prisons,* 55 DUKE L.J. 437, 544 (2005):

> [T]he state's use of private prisons reflects a larger trend toward viewing incarceration in economic terms and regarding prison inmates as the economic units of a financial plan. If anything, private prisons appear to be the logical extension of this vision, which already informs myriad aspects of this country's criminal justice system, including the practice of prison administrators contracting out the provision of basic services to cut the cost of corrections; underinvestment in mechanisms for accountability and oversight; and the tendency of private prison providers, correctional officers, and the voters themselves to look to increased incarceration as the means to their financial well-being .

[42] Lucy Komisar, *How the Food Industry Eats Your Kid's Lunch,* N.Y. TIMES, Dec. 3, 2011, http://www.nytimes.com/2011/12/04/opinion/sunday/school-lunches-and-the-food-industry.html?pagewanted=all; *see also California Food Policy Advocates & Samuels & Associates,* THE FEDERAL CHILD NUTRITION COMMODITY PROGRAM (2008), *available at* http://rwjf.org/content/dam/farm/legacy-parents/rwjf31564 (discussing the impact of the program on the nutritional quality of school meals).

[43] Komisar, *supra* note 42.

distributors) in the public sphere has a very real and negative effect on families who are at the center of the private sphere. Liz Kruger, an advocate for the poor in New York City, takes the position that: "there is something fundamentally wrong with having a for profit model for delivery of human services. Companies decide to stop unprofitable ventures. However, you still have to deliver the human services. What happens if there is no infrastructure left because you contracted out: the company either makes money and leaves the market, or does not make money and leaves, or violates the rules and is asked by government to leave. There is no infrastructure in place to continue to deliver those services."[44]

As more governmental functions are transferred from the public to the private side of the boundary, government's influence and effectiveness are diminished and private sector power is augmented. As corporations grow in size and wealth, they overwhelm the family and the public sphere. In light of this reality, an updated version of Olsen's public/private model depicted *supra* might look as follows, thereby illustrating the massive increase in the market aspect of the private sphere:

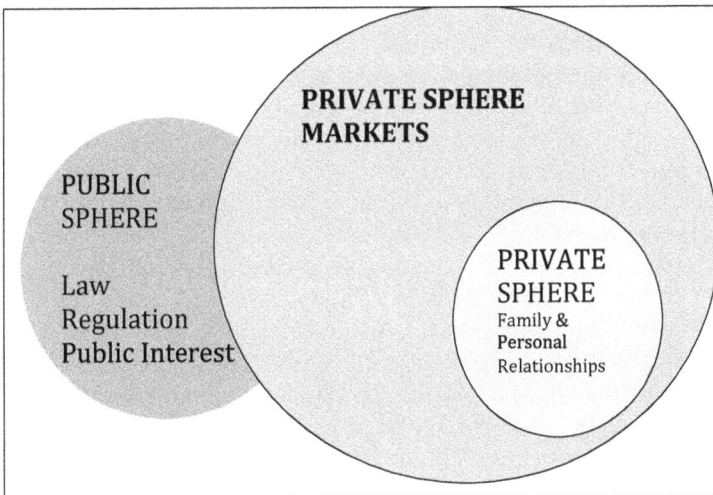

This is some of the inheritance reflected in and advanced by *Citizens United*: corporate privatization of the public sphere on every front including the electoral process. Consequently, we identify as a clear negative the collapse of any distinction between public and private though this may seem somewhat ironic from the

---

[44] *Privatization in Practice: Human Services*, 28 FORDHAM URB. L.J. 1435, 1451 (2001) (panel discussion).

perspective of certain strands of early feminism. From that vantage point, the threat to women was from the very distinction between public and private. Now the threat emerges from *elimination* of that distinction. As will be explored *infra*, part of a feminist rebuttal to *Citizens United* calls for a return to context—corporations are *not* citizens—and a reclaiming of the public sphere as distinct. This is not to suggest that *Citizens United* will be easily overturned or corporate power will fade away. But it is to suggest an aspect of the reply given by feminism(s) and the foundations of a resounding denunciation.

III. Citizens United and the Importance of Context

In 2010, the United States Supreme Court decided the case of *Citizens United v. Federal Election Commission*. It ruled that restrictions in the *Bipartisan Campaign Reform Act* of 2002 ("BCRA") on direct expenditures of funds from for-profit corporate treasuries to support or oppose candidates for political office were unconstitutional restrictions on corporations' rights to free speech.[45] As will be discussed, the Court removed restrictions on corporate donations to the electoral process thereby significantly extending private power into the public sphere and it reached this result by refusing to account for either the context out of which the case arose or the treacherous consequences that would result. This strategy of de-contextualization, in turn, commercializes and monetizes political speech by extending it—without restriction or calibration—to economic vehicles.

By way of contrast, an emphasis on context has been a tremendously important element of how feminism(s) approach legal problems. Professors Martha Minow and Elizabeth Spelman, for example, argue that "justice is more likely to be served when judges attend to the specific contexts in which their judgments are rendered."[46] They define context as a "readiness, indeed an eagerness, to recognize patterns of differences that have been used historically to distinguish among people, among places, and among problems." [47] An important background insight such feminists deploy is

---

[45] *See* Citizens United v. Fed. Election Comm'n,130 S. Ct. 876, 913 (2010).

[46] Martha Minow & Elizabeth V. Spelman, *In Context*, 63 S. Cal. L. Rev. 1597, 1598-99 (1990).

[47] *Id.* at 1600. *See also* Barbara Ann White, *Feminist Foundations for the Law of Business: One Law and Economics Scholar's Survey and (Re)view*, 10 UCLA Women's L.J. 39, 50 (1999) (noting that "contextual analysis recognizes that the prevailing social paradigm may not be meaningful for those individuals whose voices are excluded" (emphasis omitted)).

that context acts as the tool for unmasking the masculine bias in seemingly neutral legal rules, and for accounting for women's experiences in understanding the particular consequences of applying legal rules.

On a related front, Katharine Bartlett uses the term "feminist practical reasoning"[48] to describe a method of legal analysis that "builds upon the 'practical' in its focus on the specific, real-life dilemmas posed by human conflict—dilemmas that more abstract forms of legal reasoning often tend to gloss over."[49] This method gives greater attention to context and individual circumstances, rather than ignoring them in favor of reaching some form of "abstract justice."[50]

Deploying these kinds of feminist methods, commentators such as Steven Friedland have noted that certain Supreme Court justices such as Justice O'Conner—not coincidentally the first female Supreme Court justice—pay particular attention to context in arriving at a given decision while other justices neglect to do so. This impacts the quality of the opinions rendered. As Freidland notes in his analysis of *Washington v. Glucksburg*,[51] (a case which concerned a constitutional challenge to the state of Washington's ban against assisted suicide), there is a marked contrast between the abstract approach taken by Chief Justice Rehnquist and the pragmatic reasoning of Justice O'Conner. Freidland states:

> Importantly, Chief Justice Rehnquist minimized the significance of entire groups of fact through a categorical assertion about the law. . . Justice O'Connor . . .negotiated a pragmatic understanding of fact in justifying the outcome on a practical level . . .[She] not only uses such facts, but bases her avoidance of the constitutional claim on the issue of [the facts about] pain and palliative care. . . .[52]

Indeed, Justice O'Conner begins her concurrence with attention to context and individual experience: "Death will be different for

---

[48] Katharine T. Bartlett, *Feminist Legal Methods*, 103 Harv. L. Rev. 829, 854 (1990).

[49] *Id.* at 850.

[50] *Id.* at 849.

[51] Washington v. Glucksberg, 521 U.S. 702 (1997).

[52] Steven I. Friedland, The Centrality of Fact to the Judicial Perspective: Fact Use in Constitutional Cases, 35 Conn. L. Rev. 91, 125-27 (2002); *see also* Martha Minow, The Supreme Court 1986 Term—Foreword: Justice Engendered, 101 Harv. L. Rev. 10, 48-49 (1987) ("Justice O'Connor's more significant contribution may lie in her hint at a common approach to religious, racial and gender

each of us. For many, the last days will be spent in physical pain and perhaps the despair that accompanies physical deterioration and a loss of control of basic bodily and mental functions. Some will seek medication to alleviate that pain and other symptoms."[53] While agreeing with the Chief Justice that there is no general right of assisted suicide, Justice O'Connor also showed her understanding of and sensitivity to the reality in which families and caregivers find themselves by stating that "dying patients . . . can obtain palliative care, even when doing so would hasten their deaths."[54] Thus, she reaches the same conclusion as the majority, not by insisting on a bright line between Constitutional mandates concerning the continuation of life and all other possibilities, but by recognizing that each of us will have particular circumstances that may not fit such a bright line rule. Justice O'Connor's analysis is vastly superior to the alternative and a judicial emulation of her approach is much more likely to forge the right result going forward.

As the foregoing analysis suggests, feminism(s) know that acontextual and abstract judicial decisions jeopardize a just result because there is no realistic attention paid to what is actually at issue and what is actually at risk. And this is precisely where the majority decision in *Citizens United* falters and fails. As the following discussion will illustrate, the decision is fuelled by abstraction, acontextuality, and a concomitant refusal to respect even the most obvious of distinctions.

The *Citizens United* case was brought by the non-profit organization Citizens United to obtain a declaratory judgment that the corporation's airing of a documentary within 30 days of the impending primary could not be constitutionally prohibited.[55] The documentary visited critical focus on Hillary Clinton, a candidate in the democratic presidential primary. In a move that the dissent

---

based differences. Although it is an apparent aside, Justice O'Connor has in the past implicitly made an important intellectual—and normative—move: she has suggested that insights about one area of difference may be relevant and instructive to other areas of difference. Those who understand invidious messages about race or sex might thus borrow those understandings in thinking about religion. We learn by importing understandings from one context to another. Thus, in her awareness of the potential analogies across differences, and in her sensitivity to contrasting perspectives, Justice O'Connor effectively challenges the often unstated assumption that the observer can be free from a perspective. In her retention of the language of objectivity, however, she reiterates that assumption." (footnotes omitted)).

[53] *Glucksberg*, 521 U.S. at 736 (O'Connor, J., concurring).

[54] *Id.* at 738.

[55] Citizens United v. Fed. Election Comm'n, 558 U.S. 310, 321 (2010) (also seeking injunctive relief).

describes as "unusual and inadvisable"[56] the Court, on its own motion, scheduled a re-argument of the case to consider whether the
provisions of campaign laws restricting a range of corporate political activities, violated the First Amendment to the United States
Constitution by abridging the speech rights of corporations.[57] In a
five to four decision, the Court concluded that they did. According the Court, whether the speech was made by a corporation or
a natural person mattered not: corporations and natural persons
were jurisprudentially identical in relation to this aspect of the First
Amendment.[58] *Citizens United's* extension of corporate personhood into the political arena has been widely and roundly criticized,
first by the strong dissent of four of the Supreme Court Justices,[59]
and subsequently by numerous legal scholars.[60]

First and foremost, the majority in *Citizens United* was intent
on dissolving the line or distinction between the public sphere —
comprised of living, breathing citizens — and the private sphere of
market activity dominated by corporations. The goal was to trans-
form economic vehicles into American citizens entitled to fulsome
and unfettered political expression. There are many examples of

---

[56] *Id.* at 396 (Stevens, J., concurring in part and dissenting in part).

[57] *Id.* at 322 (majority opinion).

[58] *Id.* at 342-43.

[59] *Id.* at 393-479 (Stevens, J., concurring in part and dissenting in part)
(joined by Justices Ginsburg, Breyer, and Sotomayor).

[60] A representative sampling of a growing body of articles critical of the case
include: Michael S. Kang, *The End of Campaign Finance Law*, 98 VA. L. REV. 1, 4
(2012) (positing that the most significant consequences of Citizens United will
be the "doctrinal consequences for the definition of corruption as a basis for
campaign finance regulation" and the substantial narrowing of the definition of
corruption such that it no longer provides a rationale for limitations on campaign
spending that amount to anything less than a quid pro quo transaction); Jessica
A. Levinson, *We the Corporations?: The Constitutionality of Limitations on
Corporate Electoral Speech After* Citizens United, 46 U.S.F. L. REV. 307 (2011)
(arguing, contrary to the *Citizens United* holding, that the government has a
compelling interest in regulating corporate speech and proposing a regulatory
distinction between for-profit and non-profit corporations); Daniel R. Ortiz,
Recovering the Individual in Politics, 15 N.Y.U. J. LEGIS. & PUB. POL'Y 263, 287
(2012) (lamenting the Court's finding that a corporation is an "expressive
association" thereby "squeeze[ing] the individualist view completely out of
the First Amendment"); Amy J. Sepinwall, Citizens United *and the Ineluctable
Question of Corporate Citizenship*, 44 CONN. L. REV. 575 (2012) (addressing
the dilution of citizenship rights of individual citizens); Robert Sprague &
Mary Ellen Wells, *The Supreme Court as Prometheus: Breathing Life into the
Corporate Supercitizen*, 49 AM. BUS. L.J. 507 (2012) (arguing that the Court's
decision sets the stage for corporate domination of the political system).

this exercise throughout the majority's opinion, with the following statement being one of the more dramatic iterations:

> If the First Amendment has any force, it prohibits Congress from fining or jailing citizens, or associations of citizens, for simply engaging in political speech. If the antidistortion rationale were to be accepted, however, it would permit Government to ban political speech simply because the speaker is an association that has taken on the corporate form.[61]

Through the rhetoric of linkage, the majority creates in one sentence an indelible identification amongst citizens, associations of citizens, and corporations. Corporations are seen, at bottom, as simply associated citizens; they must have unfettered speech because anything less is to limit the speech of citizenry. Later in the judgment, the Court is even more direct, referring to corporations in America as "millions of associations of citizens"[62] and observing how the challenged law penalizes "certain disfavored associations of citizens—those that have taken the corporate form...."[63] In this way, market-players in the private sphere are ushered into the public realm holus bolus and untethered from regulatory oversight. The moment that profit-seeking economic vehicles are analogized to living citizens is the moment when the absolutely crucial distinction between corporate and individual campaign spending is crushed. When the majority referred to the "'open marketplace'of ideas,"[64] they were, apparently, speaking literally.

While there is room for debate on this point, it would seem that in the examples given above, the court is relying on the "aggregate" view of the corporation, a perspective which sees "the corporation as an aggregate of its members or shareholders."[65] The notion, aptly summarized by Reuven Avi-Jonah in another context, is for the court to "look through the corporation to its members"[66] and put the emphasis "entirely on the shareholders, not on the corporation itself."[67] This aggregate view is in distinction to the artificial entity theory (which sees the corporation as "a creature of the

---

[61] 558 U.S. at 349.

[62] *Id.* at 354.

[63] *Id.* at 356.

[64] *Id.* at 354 (citing N.Y. State Bd. of Elections v. Lopez Torres, 552 U.S. 196, 208 (2008)).

[65] Reuven S. Avi-Yonah, Citizens United *and the Corporate Form*, 2010 WIS. L. REV. 999, 1001 (2010).

[66] *Id.* at 1008.

[67] *Id.* at 1035.

State")[68] and the real entity theory (which regards the corporation as "a separate entity controlled by its managers").[69] In the examples above, the majority is not treating the corporation as a separate legal entity (which could therefore be subject to a different set of rules concerning electoral donations from that of individuals) but as a symbol or avatar for all the shareholders standing behind it.

Following this analysis of the decision, the court falls into theoretical inconsistency when, in other passages, it treats the corporation as a separate legal entity. For example, as Avi-Yonah observes, the majority in *Citizens United* clearly deploys the real entity theory when it stated that the statutory permissibility of a Political Action Committee or "PAC"[70] fails to obviate the limit (or "ban") on corporate speech because "[a] PAC is a separate association from the corporation."[71] As Avi-Yonah notes: "This assertion can only be made under the real entity view because under the aggregate view both the corporation and the PAC are owned by the same ultimate shareholders..."[72] Beyond this, the majority expressly rejected the argument advanced by the government that limiting corporate independent expenditures but permitting PACs is a way of protecting dissenting shareholders. In response, the Court tersely invoked *Bellotti's*[73] conclusion that dissenters who disagree with the proposed corporate political message can correct the situation "'through the procedures of corporate democracy.'"[74]

---

[68] *Id.* at 1001.

[69] *Id.*

[70] Regulation of political contributions by corporations and labor unions under 2 U.S.C. § 441(b) recognized committees commonly known as Political Action Committees or "PACs". According to Professor Richard Briffault,

> Although Citizens United referred to a PAC as 'a separate association from the corporation,' legally it is entirely controlled by the corporation that creates it. The corporation selects its officers and staff and, most importantly, the corporation can determine which candidates the PAC supports and how much money it can spend with respect to each of those candidates. The PAC is the corporation's legally authorized campaign spending alter ego, although it can spend only what it raises in voluntary donations from corporate stockholders and personnel, not from the corporation's general treasury.

Richard Briffault, *Corporations, Corruption, and Complexity: Campaign Finance after* Citizens United, 20 CORNELL J.L. & PUB. POL'Y. 643, 647-48 (2011) (footnotes omitted).

[71] Citizens United v. Fed. Election Comm'n, 558 U.S. 310, 37 (2010).

[72] Avi-Yonah, *supra* note 65, at 1040.

[73] First Nat'l Bank of Boston v. Bellotti, 435 U.S. 765 (1978).

[74] *Citizens United*, 558 U.S. at 362 (quoting Bellotti, *supra* note 73, at 794).

The majority's conclusion at this point is that the corporation is *not* simply the sum of its shareholders.

It would seem that that the Court is actually relying on more than one conceptualization of the corporation[75] depending on the argument it would like to succeed. On the one hand, the aggregate view of the corporation is *rejected* when the government offers it as a reason why the regulatory limits on corporate speech are constitutional to protect the rights of dissenting shareholders. On the other hand, the same view is *accepted* when the Court wants to cast the corporation as a structured assembly of individuals – that is, it is the aggregate of its membership. And in the majority's hands, both approaches advance privatization of the public sphere. An amorphous theoretical stance becomes a marshalling strategy which drives this conclusion: there are no relevant differences between the corporation and the individual or between corporate and individual campaign spending. As a result and as summarized by the dissent, the majority concluded that "the First Amendment precludes regulatory distinctions based on speaker identity, including the speaker's identity as a corporation."[76]

Beyond this, and as Michael Kent Curtis notes, the Court is mistaken when it regards the corporation as an association of shareholders which, when it speaks, is subject to "control by citizen shareholders."[77] Directors and executives decide when a corporation will speak and what it will say.[78] Dissenting shareholders from this speech have little to no recourse, contrary to the majority's extraordinarily general assertion to the contrary. A derivative action is possible but only to prevent future political speech and

---

[75] For discussion, see Anne Tucker, *Flawed Assumptions: A Corporate Law Analysis of Free Speech and Corporate Personhood in* Citizens United, 61 CASE W. RES. L. REV. 497, 531-34 (2011) (discussing shareholder derivative suits and shareholder proxy proposals as examples of mechanisms by which corporations recognize conflicting and diverse voices among shareholders). Note that Avi-Yonah regards the Court's reasoning as reflective of the real entity view of the corporation. Avi-Yonah, *supra* note 65, at 1040.

[76] *Citizens United*, 558 U.S. at 414 (Stevens, J., concurring in part and dissenting in part).

[77] Michael Kent Curtis, Citizens United, Davis v. FEC, *and* Arizona Free Enterprise *in Context:* Lochner *on Steroids and Democracy on Life Support*, 29 (Wake Forest Univ. Legal Studies, Working Paper No. 2029209, Apr. 5, 2012), *available at* http://papers.ssrn.com/sol3/papers.cfm?abstract_id=2029209.

[78] Lucian A. Bebchuk & Robert J. Jackson, Jr., *Corporate Political Speech: Who Decides?*, 124 HARV. L. REV. 83 (2010) ("Under existing law, a corporation's decision to engage in political speech is governed by the same rules as ordinary business decisions, which give directors and executives virtually plenary authority.") (cited by Curtis, *supra* note 77, at 29).

only if the speech were to constitute a breach of fiduciary duty or other wrong.[79] As the dissent in *Citizens United* notes, such minority challenges are "'so limited as to be almost nonexistent' given the internal authority wielded by boards and managers and the expansive protections afforded by the business judgment rule."[80] Other options for the disgruntled include voting out the board or selling their shares[81] but these are simply not realistic.[82] Dissenting shareholders by definition lack the voting power to prevail and there may be no viable way for dissenters to actually dispossess themselves of the shares in question.[83] Moreover, as Professor Benjamin Sachs points out, many shareholders who are public employees—state, local, and federal—are required to participate in pension plans. These shareholders have no access to dissenters' rights, cannot sell their shares, nor even choose the managers who speak on behalf of the corporations in which the plan invests.[84] The majority's abstract reference to "'procedures of corporate democracy'"[85] is self-serving, superficial and glib. It is utterly divorced from the context of being a minority shareholder and what that means practically speaking.

In contrast to the majority, the dissent consistently regards the corporation as distinct from its shareholders and is therefore more readily able to see the tremendous differences between a corporation and a human being. A particularly descriptive analysis is offered by Justice Stevens:

> The fact that corporations are different from human beings might seem to need no elaboration, except that the

---

[79] *See* Tucker, *supra* note 75, at 533.

[80] *Citizens United*, 558 U.S. at 477 (Stevens, J., concurring in part and dissenting in part)..

[81] *Id.* at 477-78 (Stevens, J., concurring in part and dissenting in part) (criticizing the majority's reliance on these procedures and suggesting that shareholder options are in fact quite limited).

[82] *See id.*

[83] Levinson, *supra* note 60, at 352, notes, for example, that many shareholders hold stock through intermediaries and have "little control over their shares." Beyond this, even if a shareholder disagrees with the message, the damage is done before the shareholder can sell, and, in any event, the sale may result in tax penalties. *Id.*

[84] *See* Benjamin I. Sachs, *How Pensions Violate Free Speech*, N.Y. TIMES, July 12, 2012, http://www.nytimes.com/2012/07/13/opinion/under-citizens-united-public-employees-are-compelled-to-pay-for-corporate-political-speech.html?_r=2&nl=opinion&em. Professor Sachs states that this "consequence of *Citizens United* is perverse: requiring public employees to finance corporate electoral spending amounts to compelled political speech and association, something the First Amendment flatly forbids." *Id.*

[85] *Citizens United*, 558 U.S. at 362 (*quoting* Bellotti, *supra* note 73, at 794).

majority opinion almost completely elides it...Unlike natural persons, corporations have "limited liability" for their owners and managers, "perpetual life," separation of ownership and control, "and favorable treatment of the accumulation and distribution of assets... that enhance their ability to attract capital and to deploy their resources in ways that maximize the return on their shareholders' investments." Unlike voters in U.S. elections, corporations may be foreign controlled. Unlike other interest groups, business corporations have been "effectively delegated responsibility for ensuring society's economic welfare"; they inescapably structure the life of every citizen. "'[T]he resources in the treasury of a business corporation,'" furthermore, "'are not an indication of popular support for the corporation's political ideas.'" "'They reflect instead the economically motivated decisions of investors and customers. The availability of these resources may make a corporation a formidable political presence, even though the power of the corporation may be no reflection of the power of its ideas.'"[86]

Likewise, in the words of Stevens J., "corporations have no consciences, no beliefs, no feelings, no thoughts, no desires...[T]hey are not themselves members of 'We the People' by whom and for whom our Constitution was established."[87] All this stands as an eloquent rebuttal to the analysis of the majority.

On a related front, and as William Patton and Randall Bartlett observed in a 1981 law review article, "corporations as such, do not speak or think or have ideas. Corporate actions are the *medium* of expression of those *natural* persons who control them."[88] That is, corporate managers articulate their political views through the corporate vehicle that they control. On this basis, when the majority in *Citizens United* ignores the line between public and private by admitting corporations as fully unregulated citizens, it is actually conferring "a special state-created mechanism for speaking"[89] on those individuals behind the corporation. Therefore the problem is not merely that corporations do not speak. It is that, based on the majority's analysis, some people get to speak twice — once as

---

[86] *Id.* at 465 (Stevens, J., concurring in part and dissenting in part) (internal citations omitted).

[87] *Id.* at 466.

[88] Patton & Bartlett, *supra* note 10, at 498 (emphasis in original).

[89] *Id.*

the individual speaking for himself and once as a corporate officer or director speaking for the corporation. As Charles Lindblom observes: "[t]he effect of granting the enterprise a citizen's right…is to confer great special powers on groups of enterprise executives, who can make use of corporate assets and personnel in addition to exercising the rights and powers they enjoy as individual citizens."[90]

A related point is that when corporate electoral speech is curtailed, the marketplace of ideas is not actually deprived of content, contrary to the majority view. This is because, as Levinson notes, "each individual member of a corporation, whether that corporation is a Fortune 500 or a small closed corporation, is free to speak as much as she wants without the use of the corporate form. Electioneering communications by individuals are unlimited."[91] As the dissent in *Citizens United* concludes, the rules restricting corporate speech affect only the medium by which ideas are expressed. The rules do "not prevent anyone from speaking in his or her own voice."[92]

The majority's drive to eliminate context, and its refusal to attach significance to obvious differences between citizen and corporation, lead to the creation of an impoverished, homogenous public sphere. The result is that financially powerful people can amplify their voices at the expense of the under-resourced whose voice may not be heard at all. As the dissent states:

> [T]here are substantial reasons why a legislature might conclude that unregulated general treasury expenditures will give corporations "unfai[r] influence" in the electoral process and distort public debate in ways that undermine rather than advance the interests of listeners. The legal structure of corporations allows them to amass and deploy financial resources on a scale few natural persons can match."[93]

Far from enhancing the public sphere by ostensibly inviting in more voices, the majority is actually stamping out diversity by

---

[90] CHARLES E. LINDBLOM, THE MARKET SYSTEM: WHAT IT IS, HOW IT WORKS, AND WHAT TO MAKE OF IT 239 (2002).

[91] Levinson, *supra* note 60, at 340 (footnotes omitted).

[92] *Citizens United*, 558 U.S. at 466 (Stevens, J., concurring in part and dissenting in part).

[93] *Id.* at 469 (quoting Austin v. Mich. Chamber of Commerce, 494 U.S. 652, 660 (1990)).

privileging the words of the wealthy.[94] As a result, "democratic dialogue is degraded"[95] and democracy itself is damaged.

Clearly, the majority's most egregious error in *Citizens United*
was to refuse to distinguish between individual and corporate
speech based on there being no essential distinction between citizens and corporations. But the strategy of refusing to make distinctions is repeated throughout the judgment and, in so doing, is
highly biased in favor of abstraction and one that thematically re-
jects context and consequences. For example, in contrast to the fundamental principle of judicial restraint that consciously endeavors
to find the narrowest basis for a decision[96] the majority in *Citizens
United* looked for broad rules, repelling all and every alternative
basis to decide the case. It therefore rejected an argument made in
an *amicus* brief that would have reduced the reach of the *Bipartisan
Campaign Reform Act of 2001* ("BCRA") to the benefit of Citizens
United. That is, the brief argued that the *BCRA* definition of public
transmission—a transmission that "[c]an *be received* by 50,000 or
more persons"—be construed as requiring a "plausible likelihood
that the communication will be *viewed* by 50,000 or more potential voters."[97] The latter, more reticent approach to triggering the
Act's application would have exempted Citizens United. But such
a strategy was turned down because, according to the Court, "[i]
n addition to the costs and burdens of litigation, this [approach]
would require a calculation as to the number of people a particular
communication is likely to reach, with an inaccurate estimate potentially subjecting the speaker to criminal sanctions."[98]

Next, the Court refused to decide the case based on the type
of media, stating "[w]e must decline to draw, and then redraw, constitutional lines based on the particular media or technology used
to disseminate political speech from a particular speaker."[99] Third,
the Court refused to make a distinction between for-profit and not-
for-profit corporations with regard to political expenditures. That
is, it could have concluded, on a *de minimus* basis, that Citizens
United was essentially a not-for-profit corporation and therefore
not caught by the *BCRA*. Indeed, most of Citizens United's fund-

---

[94] *Cf.* Curtis, *supra* note 77, at 13 (discussing the ecology of freedom of
speech and democracy in these terms).

[95] *Id.* at 19.

[96] *See Citizens United*, 559 U.S. at 398-99 (Stevens, J., concurring in part and
dissenting in part).

[97] *Id.* at 323 (majority opinion) (internal quotation and citation omitted)
(emphasis added).

[98] *Id.* at 324.

[99] *Id.* at 326.

ing came from its private donors who are presumably aligned with its positions only a small percentage of its funding came from for-profit corporations. In refusing to apply a *de minimus* standard to the corporation at bar, the Court stated: "[w]e decline to adopt an interpretation that requires intricate case-by-case determinations to verify whether political speech is banned, especially if we are convinced that, in the end, this corporation has a constitutional right to speak on this subject."[100] In this way, the Court summarily dismissed significant distinctions between for-profit and non-profit corporations. The reality is that many non-profit corporations are established for the very purpose of aligning the interests of their private donors with positions on public issues[101] whereas for-profit corporations are interested maximizing the investments of share-holders and returning profits in the form of increased value to shareholders.

The Court also had the opportunity to rely on Federal Election Commission regulations[102] as they apply to requests for advisory opinions to manage a *de minimus* exception that would cover non-profits that receive a small percentage of their funding from for-profit organizations. Again the Court found that to act on a case by case basis was simply too complex and burdensome. In short, such a regulatory requirement amounted to a prior restraint on speech.[103] And in a catch-all rejection of context in favor of a broad, abstract rule, the Court determined that "[t]here are short timeframes in which speech can have influence" and thus, there is no time to litigate the particulars of each case.[104]

Feminism(s)—with its focus on context—can easily see through all of this and delineate the serious problems inherent in the Court's approach. As explained above, the majority's strategy is to deny distinctions and to deny the possibility that distinctions could ever be constitutionally made. The majority guts the

---

[100] *Id.* at 329.

[101] Levinson, *supra* note 60, at 353 ("[w]hen . . . non-profit corporations speak, the corporations' electoral speech can be traced to the speech of the members of the corporation").

[102] 11 C.F.R. §112.4 (2012).

[103] *See Citizens United*, 558 U.S. at 335 (finding that the FEC would in effect be making such case by case determinations because most speakers would seek advisory opinions).

[104] *Id.* at 334.

legislation in question and transfers ownership of the public realm to private, monied, financial interests.

Indeed, granting unlimited free speech rights to all corporations regardless of their source of funding provides a second avenue for corporate interests to dominate the political discourse. As reporters Mike McIntire and Nicholas Confessore of the *New York Times* observed:

> Two years after the Supreme Court's *Citizens United* decision opened the door for corporate spending on elections, relatively little money has flowed from company treasuries into "super PACs," which can accept unlimited contributions but must also disclose donors. Instead, there is growing evidence that large corporations are trying to influence campaigns by donating money to tax-exempt organizations that can spend millions of dollars without being subject to the disclosure requirements that apply to candidates, parties and PACs. [105]

This lack of scrutiny creates a tremendous danger by allowing corporations to essentially have it both ways. It is having it both ways when corporations are accorded the power to give unlimited financial donations in a political context but are not simultaneously required to disclose their large, monied presence in the debate at issue. In arguing for disclosure of donors to tax exempt organizations, Alex Engler, of the Georgetown Public Policy Review, notes that Super-PACs and their sister tax-exempt organizations account for a large market share of political contributions, and their dual structure that offers donor anonymity is an "appealing choice for... corporate interests that want to avoid political fallout."[106]

In short, *Citizens United* manifests an egregious decision inexorably propelled by an egregious judicial strategy. To conclude that corporations have the First Amendment rights of an individual citizen, the Court had to erase a host of distinctions that would point in the opposite direction. This erasure includes: the distinction between corporate aggregations of wealth from many people and the wealth of individuals (because the Court disregards the nature of the speaker altogether); the distinction between managers who make decisions to expend funds from the corporate treasury and corporation itself (because the corporation's right to speak is

---

[105] McIntire & Confessore, *supra* note 8.

[106] Alex Engler, *Sunshine for the Super PAC: The DISCLOSE Act Would Eliminate Anonymous Donors*, GEORGETOWN PUB. POL'Y REV. (2012), *available at* http://gppreview.com/2012/04/05/sunshine-for-the-super-pacl.

"CAN YOU HEAR ME NOW...GOOD!"®

disconnected from those who control the content and dissemination of the message); the distinction between media corporations and other corporations (because the Court refused to recognize the historic role of the media which stand in a special relationship to the First Amendment); and the distinction between banning speech and merely regulating it.[107] The stripped down, abstract universe that the majority generates inexorably produces a privatized public sphere, that is a sphere that the Court places in the hands of private economic interests. Those whose voices have been historically marginalized—including women's voices—will be excluded from the political and policy making arena more than ever before.

IV. FEMINIST RESPONSES TO CITIZENS

Criticism of the ruling in *Citizens United* was immediate and quickly abundant. Two commentators in particular, Atiba Ellis and Robin West, illustrate how the tools of feminism (which *inter alia* illuminate the underlying domination that abstraction serves to perpetuate) are central to understanding the impact of *Citizens United* and how it can be redialed.

Ellis cites two consequences of the *Citizens United* decision to clothe corporations with political personhood. First, as already noted in the previous section, the ruling gives corporations the opportunity to exercise unprecedented, unlimited influence and control over the country's political discourse.[108] Second, the corporate dominance created by *Citizens United* will affirm the relative power of historically privileged white males over other groups.[109] Ellis concludes that "[t]his new era of corporate rights dominating the rights of natural persons may lead to a new period of tiered legal personhood in our democracy, an outcome that is inconsistent with the vision of rights under our modern Constitution."[110] In addition to this, she notes that *Citizens United* requires us to consider the interrelationship of ideas that deserve further exposition, including the interrelationship between the mobilization of capital and the protection of status.[111] When viewed through the lens of the public/

---

[107] As the dissent notes, "the majority invokes the specter of a 'ban' on nearly every page of its opinion. This characterization is highly misleading, and needs to be corrected." *Citizens United*, 558 U.S. at 416 (Stevens, J., concurring in part and dissenting in part) (internal citation omitted).

[108] *See* Atiba R. Ellis, Citizens United *and Tiered Personhood*, 44 J. MARSHALL. L. REV. 717, 745-46 (2011).

[109] *See id.* at 747-49.

[110] *Id.* at 726.

[111] *Id.* at 745 n.132.

private dichotomy, Ellis's criticisms of *Citizens United* very much resonate. They illustrate that the public/private divide has been breached—though not in the way that feminists like MacKinnon, discussed earlier, had argued for. Instead of making the private the public to reduce the oppression of women, *Citizens United* makes the public into the private so as to serve corporate purposes. It pushes a traditionally public arena, the electoral college, into the private realm. *Citizens United* portends that the oppression that characterized women's experiences in the private sphere can now be more readily imposed in the public sphere by those who can economically dominate it. The private is now the public.

Similarly and in light of *Citizens United*, Robin West calls for a revitalization of the rights critique that characterized critical legal theory,[112] including feminist theory, until the early 1990s.[113] Like Ellis, West sees the decision in *Citizens United* as an example of subordination of the powerless by the powerful.[114] When the U.S. Supreme Court granted electioneering communication rights to corporations, this did not make corporations merely equal to human speakers. Rather, the newly vested corporate right to political speech exists in relation of the speech rights of others whose ability to speak is vastly underfunded and who have diminished or no political access. Though there is no reference to the public/private distinction in her article, West offers an approach that is implicitly consistent with the public private analysis offered here. In short, when the public sphere is dominated by powerful private interests, the distinction between public and private dissolves. This leaves women and other disadvantaged groups highly vulnerable.

A third theorist, Michael Siebecker, proposes to respond to *Citizens United* with a new discourse theory of the firm.[115] Siebecker recognizes the increasing corporate dominance that is likely to result from *Citizens United*,[116] predicting that "the ability to direct

---

[112] Critical legal theories, described by Ellis, see the law as the outgrowth of power relationships in society, and a tool for those with power to maintain it at the expense of those who are powerless. Ellis, *supra* note 108, at 722 n.23.

[113] Robin L. West, *Tragic Rights: The Rights Critique in the Age of Obama*, 53 WM. & MARY L. REV. 713 (2011); *accord* Ellis, *supra* note 108, at 722 n.23 ("the jurisprudential ramifications of *Citizens United* should be viewed through the lenses of Critical Legal Studies (CLS) and, more specifically, Critical Race Theory (CRT) and Feminist Legal Theory").

[114] West, *supra* note 113, at 723 ("[i]t is hard to doubt that . . . extending speech rights to corporations to influence political elections subordinates individual to corporate interests").

[115] Michael R. Siebecker, *A New Discourse Theory of the Firm After* Citizens United, 79 GEO. WASH. L. REV. 161 (2010).

[116] *Id.* at 169-179. Siebecker is also responding to a new SEC Rule 14a-11

corporate decisions represents the ability to control political life."[117] With regard to the relative effectiveness of the public and private spheres of influence, Siebecker argues that "the private boardroom rather than the public forum represents the relevant battlefield for determining the most important aspects of our lives."[118]

The discourse theory attempts to move the principles of public participation to the corporation to address public issues. The theory focuses on the effectiveness of organizational structures that affect society, which requires communicative actions with full, fair and free participation through procedures that make the outcomes legitimate.[119] According to Siebecker, discourse theory protects individual rights by encouraging participation and providing a sense of fairness, for example, by giving shareholders the right to include their nominees for directors in corporate proxy materials.[120] Increased private power requires increased private democracy.

Siebecker believes that applying a discourse theory to public decision making will justify limitations on the effects of *Citizens*.[121] But in doing so, he brings into sharp focus the very problem that the case has created. Discourse theory falls short because it requires those opposed to *Citizens United* to cede so much ground, including the ongoing privatization of the public sphere. For this reason, discourse theory cannot be the only front upon which to resist *Citizens*. The power structure it reflects and advances must also be attacked. If not, discourse theory becomes an apology for the perpetuation and expansion of the power of a white male dominated corporate hierarchy.

It is well known that the power structure of corporate America is not female friendly by any means. For example, a 2008 study sponsored by Ernst & Young[122] found that:

> In 2008, women held 15.7 percent of corporate officer positions at *Fortune* 500 companies; in 2007, this number

---

that gives shareholders access for corporate proxy for nominating directors, as required by Dodd-Frank. *Id.* at 210. While this increased shareholder participation is important to the discourse theory, it is outside the scope of this essay.

[117] *Id.* at 165.

[118] *Id.* at 169.

[119] *Id.* at 199.

[120] *Id.* at 204, 228-29. In July, 2011 the D.C. Circuit vacated a rule that would have made such proxy access for qualifying shareholders mandatory. *See* Business Roundtable v. SEC, 647 F.3d 1144, 1156 (D.C. Cir. 2011).

[121] Siebeker, *supra* note 115, at 197-98.

[122] *2008 Catalyst Census of Women Corporate Officers and Top Earners of the Fortune 500*, CATALYST (Dec. 2008), *available at* http://www.catalyst.org/

was 15.4 percent. Women held 6.2 percent of top earner positions; in 2007, this number was 6.7 percent. The number of companies with no women corporate officers increased from 74 in 2007 to 75 in 2008. The number of companies with three or more women corporate officers also increased from 203 in 2007 to 206 in 2008.[123]

Another study of public corporations in Georgia found that fewer than 10% of seats on boards are held by women[124] and fewer than 10% of executive officers are women.[125] The situation for women of color is even more egregious. One study in 2011 showed that approximately 71% of Fortune 500 companies had no women of color serving on their boards, and that overall, only 3% of directors of the remaining 30% were women of color.[126]

The very large absence "of women's participation at senior levels of corporate decision making," observes Janis Sarra, "means an important set of governance perspectives is lost."[127] It also means that women's voices will continue to be lost as corporations decide how to deploy their recently acquired "citizenship" power. Women's issues in the public sector are likely to get even less attention. To the extent that these issues get attention, the corporate view will not necessarily reflect the perspective of women affected by the policy.

A feminist response to *Citizens United* is now even more urgent in light of the recent ruling in *American Tradition Partnership, Inc., v. Bullock*.[128] In this 2012 decision, the U.S. Supreme Court refused an opportunity to reconsider *Citizens United*, and instead, expanded its reach into the states. The majority, in a *per curiam* opinion, again refused to consider the particular context of the case, rejecting out of hand Montana's argument that given the

---

publication/283/2008-catalyst-census-of-women-corporate-officers-and-top-earners-of-the-fortune-500.

[123] *Id.*

[124] *More Than Half-A Milestone: 2011 Board of Directors Annual Study,* BOARD OF DIRECTORS NETWORK (Oct. 14, 2011), http://www.boarddirectorsnetwork.org/docs/2011_study.pdf.

[125] *Id.*

[126] *Women on Boards,* CATALYST (Aug. 2012), http://www.catalyst.org/publication/433/. Catalyst is a non-profit organization that supports and promotes opportunities for women in business (www.catalyst.org). *See generally* Seletha R. Butler, *All on Board! Strategies for Constructing Diverse Boards of Directors,* 7 VA. L. & BUS. REV. 61 (2012) (arguing the necessity of diversity in leadership of U.S. companies and suggesting solutions for building diverse boards of directors).

[127] Sarra, *supra* note 11, at 485.

[128] 132 S. Ct. 2490 (2012) (*per curiam*).

state's unique history in relation to political corruption, the State had a compelling interest in limiting independent expenditures by corporations.[129]

V. BRIEF CONCLUSIONS

Citizens United offers a high water mark in privatizing the public sphere and refusing to consider its tangible consequences. Obsessed with the analogy of citizens and corporations, the Supreme Court refused to see obvious distinctions and assess context. In this way, the Court extended private market power into the public sphere, giving corporate interests the opportunity to financially dominate America's political process, both federally and at the state level.

Feminism(s) reply to the majority decision is simple: a just decision is stifled by a series of abstractions. Context must be considered at the front end of the analytic exercise and this would require the majority to acknowledge facts that distinguish corporations from other speakers; non-profit from for-profit corporations; associations of individuals and entities that are separate from the individuals who own them. Context must also be considered at the back end so that what emerges is a sensible appreciation of what privatizing the public sector would actually mean. Unwilling to explore this terrain, the majority refused to acknowledge these obvious conclusions: privatization diminishes the agency of human citizens whose voices in the public debate are not amplified by huge aggregations of wealth, and privatization further diminishes the power of under represented groups who do not participate to the same extent as white males in the corporate board room and whose voices are now even more muted. Privatization kills the public sphere.

One historic challenge for feminists has been to break down the barrier between public and private, in order to remove the shield of privacy from the systemic domination of women. In the wake of *Citizens United*, feminists face a new challenge: to reclaim the public from the private corporate interests and make it distinct again.

Until now, none of the commentators on *Citizens United v. FEC* have viewed the case in the context of the public/private dichotomy that is at the core of feminist jurisprudence. It is our hope that this essay can begin to fill that void and that, beyond this, feminism(s) in its various fora and manifesting all its perspectival

---

[129] *Id.* at 2491 (Breyer, J., dissenting).

diversity will demand that the public sphere be returned to the living and breathing citizens of America. We join Mae Quinn in imagining "a feminist future [in which our work is] both more practical and more radical—in a way that abdicates absolute definitions, seeks to bridge divides, and provides some semblance of substantive justice for individual people in their individual lives."[130] Feminisms(s) have the insights and methodologies to speak out against privatization and the corporate domination of public policy debates. This is also part of the way forward.

---

[130] Mae C. Quinn, *Feminist Legal Realism*, 35 HARV. J.L. & GENDER 1, 55 (2012). On a related front, Barbara Ann White has advocated the application of feminist analysis to problems that were not considered traditional feminist concerns. She wrote:

> It is evident then that feminist analysis can address issues far broader than solely women's concerns. It is also clear that feminist analysis is not limited to gender concerns, group disenfranchisement, or analyses of patriarchal hierarchy and dominance... [An analysis of the works of feminist scholars addressing business law issues] [s]hows that the principles of feminist reasoning—recognizing the excluded voice, the perspective of the other, dichotomization of social order into different spheres—can be used to uncover core problems in business law that have nothing to do with traditional gender issues.

White, *supra* note 47, at 96-97.

WHAT IS AN "UNDUE BURDEN"? THE *CASEY* STANDARD AS APPLIED TO INFORMED CONSENT PROVISIONS

Lauren Paulk*

I. INTRODUCTION

The right to an abortion remains a hotly contested area of politics. However, advocates challenging laws that restrict access to abortion do not always raise all the possible challenges, which results in a mixed application of standards by the courts. This article explores the so-called "undue burden" standard handed down by the United States Supreme Court and how lower federal courts use this standard to analyze legislation related to the right to choose.

* CUNY School of Law, J.D. expected 2013. The author wishes to thank Professor Ruthann Robson for her comments, kind encouragement to publish, and inspirational scholarship and teaching; Professor Caitlin Borgmann for early guidance, continued engagement with me about reproductive justice and the law, and for leading excellent classroom discussions that provided the impetus for this piece; *UCLA Women's Law Journal* editors and staff for their thoughtful notes and edits; and my colleagues at CUNY, whose friendship and support make law school not only bearable, but enjoyable.

First, this article will outline the history of the standard, followed by a discussion of how the Supreme Court has applied it in three major cases. Next, this article will analyze how the lower federal courts use the standard by focusing on its application to "informed consent" provisions of abortion regulation. Specifically, this article will analyze court decisions that rule on the constitutionality of legislative provisions related to pre-abortion ultrasounds and fetal pain. Finally, this article will discuss what recent applications of the undue burden standard in informed consent provisions may mean for the standard itself and for abortion rights in general. I conclude that the undue burden standard should be clarified and strengthened. Advocates should always raise the standard to help ensure courts address it. As such, challenges under the standard should run parallel to any other challenges.

Specifically, in informed consent cases, advocates should argue that the analysis under the undue burden standard begins by assessing whether the provision is truthful and not misleading.[1] If the provision is found to be truthful and not misleading, advocates should argue that the next step is whether the provision has the "purpose or effect of placing a substantial obstacle in the path of a woman who seeks an abortion of a nonviable fetus."[2] In advocating under the purpose prong, advocates should cite to legislative history and statements made by politicians that could be reasonably construed to show that the provision has the "purpose" of "hinder[ing]" a woman's free choice to abort a nonviable fetus.[3] In advocating under the effects prong, advocates should attempt to show how the large fraction test proves that the restriction is a substantial obstacle

---

[1] Planned Parenthood of Se. Pa.v. Casey, 505 U.S. 833, 882 (1992).

[2] *Id.* at 877.

[3] *Id.* However, as commentators have noted, the purpose prong of *Casey* has been relatively "neglected." Note, *After* Ayotte: *The Need to Defend Abortion Rights with Renewed "Purpose,"* 119 HARV. L. REV. 2552, 2566 (2006) [hereinafter *After* Ayotte]. Indeed, members of the Court themselves are divided in how—and whether—the purpose prong should be used. When Justice Ginsburg implied support for a disjunctive test (or the separation of "purpose" and "effect" in the *Casey* standard) in a concurrence, Justice Thomas argued back that Ginsburg's notion was "squarely inconsistent" with precedent. *See id.* at 2566-67 (quoting Stenberg v. Carhart, 530 U.S. 914, 952 (2000)). Additionally, the Court has refused to grant *certiorari* to a petition attempting to clarify how to construe the purpose prong. *See id.* at 2567 n.87 (citing Petition for Writ of Certiorari, Wood v. Univ. of Utah Med. Ctr., 540 U.S. 946 (2003) (No. 03-82), 2003 WL 22428547 (presenting the question, "[d]oes the standard for determining whether a statute has a constitutionally improper purpose under *Casey* require an examination of the entire legislative context"); *Wood*, 540 U.S. at 946 (denying certiorari)).

for a large fraction of the women for which it is relevant.[4] Finally, advocates should argue for the application of the standard to all informed consent provisions—both those already in operation in the State and those proposed in the legislation at issue—such that the provisions combined create a substantial obstacle. Even these stronger iterations of the standard, however, will only slow (at best) the introduction of new and more restrictive measures on abortion.[5]

II. A History of the Undue Burden Standard

Prior to *Roe v. Wade*, the United States Supreme Court had not grounded the right of privacy in any one constitutional provision.[6] The discussion of privacy began, however, in 1965, when *Griswold v. Connecticut* affirmed the right of married couples to use contraception.[7] A majority of the Court in *Griswold* found a "zone of privacy"[8] to exist in the marital bedroom, but placed the right in the "penumbras" that are "formed by emanations" from various constitutional provisions.[9] The *Griswold* Court did not situate this zone of privacy in any one constitutional provision; rather, Justice Douglas located it in no less than five separate constitutional amendments.[10] The Court may not have intended for its holding in

---

[4] *Casey*, 505 U.S. at 895.

[5] Still, in the current political climate, slowing down "the other side" is sometimes the last line of defense against retrogressive policies. It is questionable whether or not the courts are the place for this, but hopefully a strengthened standard on the Court would help withstand attacks from an increasingly virulent anti-choice legislative contingency.

[6] It is contested that a specific "right to privacy" was even articulated here. *See* Ruthann Robson, *Lesbians and Abortion*, 35 N.Y.U. Rev. L. & Soc. Change 247, 249 (2011) ("The word 'privacy' is not in the text of the Constitution and the Court in *Griswold* had a difficult time grounding the right in any specific constitutional provision. Justice Douglas famously opined that 'specific guarantees in the Bill of Rights have penumbras, formed by emanations from those guarantees that help give them life and substance.' The first case in which a majority of the United States Supreme Court agreed that 'privacy' was grounded in the liberty guarantee of the Due Process Clause of the Fourteenth Amendment was *Roe v. Wade*, [410 U.S. 113 (1973)] the case in which the Court first held that a state statute criminalizing abortion was unconstitutional." (footnotes omitted)). *But cf.* Lackland H. Bloom, Jr., *The Legacy of* Griswold, 16 Ohio N.U. L. Rev. 511, 512 (1989) ("If *Griswold* is remembered for one thing, it is surely for having effectively given birth to the concept of an independent constitutional right of privacy.").

[7] Griswold v. Connecticut, 381 U.S. 479, 485-86 (1965).

[8] *Id.* at 485.

[9] *Id.* at 484.

[10] *See id.* (finding zones of privacy in the First, Third, Fourth, Fifth, and Ninth Amendments).

Griswold to help establish a woman's right to choose an abortion.[11] Even so, after *Eisenstadt v. Baird* extended the right to contraception to unmarried individuals,[12] *Roe v. Wade* was not far behind.[13]

In establishing the right of unmarried persons to obtain contraception, *Eisenstadt* expanded the "zone of privacy" outside the sphere of the marital bedroom and into the lives of individuals. One year later, *Roe* firmly located the individual right to privacy (in the abortion context) in the Due Process Clause of the Fourteenth Amendment,[14] establishing a woman's right to have a pre-viability abortion if she chose.[15] *Roe* provided the governing standard for abortion rights until 1992, when *Planned Parenthood v. Casey* articulated a new standard by which abortion rights are now measured.[16]

Since the Court in *Roe* found that abortion fell under the fundamental right to privacy,[17] it applied a strict scrutiny analysis,[18] requiring that regulations be narrowly tailored to achieve a compelling state interest.[19] The *Roe* court decided that the government had two compelling interests: "preserving and protecting the health of the pregnant woman" and "protecting the potentiality of human life."[20] These interests, however, became compelling at different times during a woman's pregnancy. While the first trimester was to remain free of government interference,[21] a woman's health became a compelling state interest in the second trimester, and potential life became a compelling state interest at viability.[22] The Court gave

---

[11] *See* Robert M. Godzeno, Note, *The Role of Ultrasound Imaging in Informed Consent Legislation Post*-Gonzales v. Carhart, 27 QUINNIPIAC L. REV. 285, 288 (2009).

[12] Eisenstadt v. Baird, 405 U.S. 438, 453 (1972).

[13] Roe v. Wade, 410 U.S. 113 (1973).

[14] *See* Robson, *supra* note 6, at 249.

[15] *See Roe*, 410 U.S. at 153.

[16] *See* Planned Parenthood of Se. Pa. v. Casey, 505 U.S. 833, 877 (1992).

[17] *Roe*, 410 U.S. at 154.

[18] The foreshadowing of strict scrutiny can be found in the famous "footnote four" of United States v. Carolene Products Co., 304 U.S. 144, 152 n.4 (1938). For a more complete description of strict scrutiny, see generally 16A AM. JUR. 2D *Constitutional Law* § 403 (2012).

[19] *Roe*, 410 U.S. at 155.

[20] *Id.* at 162-63.

[21] *Id.* at 163.

[22] *Id.* at 163-64. The *Roe* Court explained that viability is the point at which the fetus can potentially sustain life outside the mother's womb, which generally occurs between twenty-four to twenty-eight weeks of pregnancy. *Id.* at 160. This definition may prove problematic in the future with advances in medical technology used to keep increasingly premature infants alive outside of the womb. *See* City of Akron v. Akron Ctr. for Reprod. Health, 462 U.S. 416, 458 (1983) (O'Connor, J., dissenting).

the states permission to ban abortion after viability due to their interest in potential life, as long as they provided a life and health exception for the mother.[23]

Therefore, the right to abortion was ensconced in the fundamental right to privacy.[24] Although in the history of Supreme Court jurisprudence all fundamental rights are typically accorded a strict scrutiny analysis,[25] abortion has since received a different standard—the "undue burden" test. In *City of Akron v. Akron Center for Reproductive Health, Inc.,*[26] Justice Sandra Day O'Connor first articulated an early version of this test. O'Connor's undue burden analysis provided that abortion regulations should only be struck down when the regulations put an "undue burden" on a woman's right to choose a pre-viability abortion.[27] This standard set the stage for *Planned Parenthood v. Casey*'s new articulation of a test for abortion restrictions.

In 1992, the *Casey* court, citing O'Connor's earlier undue burden language,[28] adopted a modified version of the undue burden standard.[29] Though *Casey* affirmed *Roe* in that it maintained that

---

[23] *Roe*, 410 U.S. at 163-64.

[24] *Id.* at 154.

[25] *See, e.g.,* Griswold v. Connecticut, 381 U.S. 479, 485-86 (1965) (applying strict scrutiny to married couple's use of contraceptives after holding that this falls under the fundamental right to privacy).

[26] O'Connor first suggested using an undue burden standard in her dissenting opinions in *Akron Ctr. for Reprod. Health*, 462 U.S. at 461-66 (O'Connor, J., dissenting), and Planned Parenthood Ass'n of Kan. City, Mo., Inc. v. Ashcroft, 462 U.S. 476, 505 (1983) (O'Connor, J., dissenting), and she continued to argue for its use in subsequent cases. The Court did use the term "undue burden" in some post-*Roe*, pre-*Casey* cases involving abortion, but there is debate over whether this term was used as a formal standard at the time. *See* Gillian E. Metzger, *Unburdening the Undue Burden Standard: Orienting* Casey *in Constitutional Jurisprudence*, 94 COLUM. L. REV. 2025, 2036-37 (1994).

[27] *Akron Ctr. for Reprod. Health*, 462 U.S. at 461-64 (O'Connor, J., dissenting). For a thorough discussion of O'Connor's pre-*Casey* articulation of the undue burden standard, see generally Susan R. Estrich & Kathleen M. Sullivan, *Abortion Politics: Writing for an Audience of One*, 138 U. PA. L. REV. 119 (1989); *see also* Metzger, *supra* note 26, at 2036 (noting that O'Connor's earlier articulations of the standard defined an undue burden as an "absolute obstacle."). Moreover, O'Connor's early version of the test deemed it a threshold inquiry, not a final standard—strict scrutiny would only be applied after an undue burden was found. *See id.*

[28] *See* Planned Parenthood of Se. Pa. v. Casey, 505 U.S. 833, 874 (1992) (citing eight prior abortion decisions, including six that are dissenting or concurring opinions by Justice O'Connor).

[29] *Casey* states that "an undue burden is an unconstitutional burden." *Id.* at 877. *But cf. Akron Ctr. for Reprod. Health*, 462 U.S. at 463-64 (O'Connor, J., dissenting) (articulating an undue burden as an "absolute obstacle"); Metzger,

women have the right to choose an abortion pre-viability,[30] the undue burden standard gave greater deference to state legislatures by allowing restrictions on abortion throughout pregnancy.[31] Under *Casey*, a state's reasons for an abortion restriction no longer have to be "compelling," nor does the restriction's tailoring need to be "narrow." Instead, *Casey* only requires that the restrictions do not constitute an undue burden.[32] An undue burden has the "purpose or effect of placing a substantial obstacle in the path of a woman seeking an abortion of a nonviable fetus."[33] Therefore, the Court created an entirely new standard by which to measure this subset of fundamental rights.[34]

In creating this standard, the Court used circular logic, leaving state and federal courts to their own devices in interpreting the

---

supra note 26, at 2036-37.

[30] *Casey*, 505 U.S. at 870; *see also* Linda J. Wharton, Susan Frietsche, & Kathryn Kolbert, *Preserving the Core of* Roe: *Reflections on* Planned Parenthood v. Casey, 18 YALE J.L. & FEMINISM 317, 329 (2006) (describing the "three central tenets" of the *Roe* decision upheld by the *Casey* Court).

[31] *Compare* Roe v. Wade, 410 U.S. 113, 163 (1973) (finding that the decision about abortion in the first trimester was between a woman and her doctor, that restrictions regarding women's health were acceptable in the second trimester, and that all other restrictions were acceptable after viability) *with Casey*, 505 U.S. at 777 (holding that restrictions throughout pregnancy are constitutional as long as they do not pose an undue burden).

[32] *Casey*, 505 U.S. at 877.

[33] *Id.*

[34] *Cf.* Turner v. Safley, 482 U.S. 78 (1987) (modifying the fundamental rights analysis in the prison context). In *Turner*, the Court ruled that, "when a prison regulation impinges on inmates' constitutional rights, the regulation is valid if it is reasonably related to legitimate penological interests .... Subjecting the day-to-day judgments of prison officials to an inflexible strict scrutiny analysis would seriously hamper their ability to anticipate security problems and to adopt innovative solutions to the intractable problems of prison administration." *Id.* at 89. Therefore, the *Turner* Court justifies modifying the strict scrutiny analysis because of the high security concerns that exist in the context of a prison. One could propose that the Court has changed the way it views the liberty interest of both prisoners and pregnant women, restricting one and expanding the other. In this sense, by foregoing strict scrutiny in the Due Process privacy and liberty right to choose, the Court is making the moral decision to place convicted criminals and pregnant women on the same plane when regarding the State's rights to interfere with an individual's bodily autonomy. *Cf.* Kim Shayo Buchanan, *The Sex Discount*, 57 UCLA L. REV. 1149 (2010) (arguing that the Court treats liberty interests differently when "illicit" sex is involved); Kim Shayo Buchanan, Lawrence v. Geduldig: *Regulating Women's Sexuality*, 56 EMORY L.J. 1235, 1281 (2007) (noting that many regulations involving (hetero) sex are purportedly designed to "protect women, not to harm them"). This is— at least in the case of informed consent provisions—why the Court allows the state to interfere with pregnant women's liberty interests. *See* Maya Manian,

constitutionality of abortion regulations. Instead of defining an undue burden, the Court chose to explain it by saying that a finding of an undue burden is "shorthand for the conclusion that a state regulation has the purpose or effect of placing a substantial obstacle in the path of a woman seeking an abortion of a nonviable fetus."[35] Problematically, the court chose not to further define "substantial obstacle," which leaves lower courts with very little guidance.[36] As Neal Devins notes in his article *How Planned Parenthood v. Casey (Pretty Much) Settled the Abortion Wars*, for some time this vague explanation did not prove much of an issue, since many states simply modeled their abortion laws after the Pennsylvania statute analyzed in *Casey*.[37] However, as this Article later explores, in recent years some states have been pushing the boundaries of the original Pennsylvania statute.[38] They have done so not only by enacting laws that are increasingly more restrictive than and dissimilar to the regulations in *Casey*, but by flouting the "purpose" aspect of the undue burden standard.[39]

III. The Scope of Constitutional Restrictions Under the Undue Burden Standard

In *Casey*, the new undue burden standard proved quite permissive as applied to a number of abortion restrictions. Applying

---

The Irrational Woman: Informed Consent and Abortion Decision-Making, 16 Duke J. Gender L. & Pol'y 223, 247-49 (2009) (outlining the historical evolution and persistence of informed consent laws).

[35] *Casey*, 505 U.S. at 877. For a comprehensive explanation of the substantial obstacle/undue burden framework, *see* Caitlin E. Borgmann, *Winter Count: Taking Stock of Abortion Rights After* Casey *and* Carhart, 31 Fordham Urb. L.J. 675, 682-89 (2004). For a critique of the undue burden standard, we need look no further than *Casey* itself, where Justice Scalia pointed out the inconsistencies inherent in the standard. *See Casey*, 505 U.S. at 987-93 (Scalia, J., concurring in part and dissenting in part) (critiquing the circular nature of the standard, which is "rootless [and]...plucked out of context from our earlier abortion decisions," and bemoaning the loss of the stronger adjectives used by O'Conner in her earlier iterations of the standard and the downgrading of the state's interest from compelling to substantial).

[36] *See Casey* 505 U.S. at 987-93 (Scalia, J., concurring in the judgment in part and dissenting in part).

[37] Neal Devins, *How* Planned Parenthood v. Casey *(Pretty Much) Settled the Abortion Wars*, 118 Yale L.J. 1318, 1338-39 (2009).

[38] *See* Wharton et al., *supra* note 30, at 319-21 (discussing the type and number of restrictions states passed from 1992-2005, as compared to the pre-*Casey* years of 1985-1991).

[39] The Court declares that an undue burden has "the *purpose* or effect of placing a substantial obstacle in the path of a woman seeking an abortion," and

the undue burden analysis, the Court found that a 24-hour waiting period,[40] parental consent for minors,[41] an informed consent provision,[42] and certain reporting requirements for medical facilities[43] were all constitutionally permissible restrictions on abortion. The Court did find one restriction unconstitutional, and in doing so used yet another modification of the undue burden analysis. The restriction that required women to notify their husbands before getting an abortion was struck down as imposing an undue burden for a "large fraction" of the women to which it applied.[44] However, this was the only restriction for which the Court employed the "large fraction" test. Therefore, the Court revealed the undue burden standard to be malleable[45] by using the "large fraction" test to strike down the husband notification provision while not addressing this test in

---

"the means chosen by the State to further the interest in potential life must be calculated to inform the woman's free choice, not hinder it." *Casey*, 505 U.S. at 877 (emphasis added). *See also* Gonzales v. Carhart, 550 U.S. 124, 160 (2007) (rejecting the argument that the congressional purpose of the legislation was not to impose an obstacle to abortion); *but see* Caroline Burnett, *Dismantling* Roe *Brick by Brick—The Unconstitutional Purpose Behind the Federal Partial-Birth Abortion Act of 2003*, 42 U.S.F. L. Rev. 227, 251-254 (2007), for an articulation of the evidence that the legislation was enacted with the purpose of putting a substantial obstacle in the path of a woman seeking an abortion. Some commentators, however, declare this aspect of the undue burden standard to have little weight. *See, e.g.*, Caitlin E. Borgmann, *Holding Legislatures Constitutionally Accountable Through Facial Challenges*, 36 Hastings Const. L.Q. 563, 578-79 (2009). *But see* Note, *After* Ayotte, *supra* note 3, at 2566-69 (acknowledging the "agnostic" language in Mazurek toward the purpose prong, but arguing for its reinvigoration); Gillian E. Metzger, *Abortion, Equality, and Administrative Regulation*, 56 Emory L.J. 865, 892, n.124 (2007) (noting that courts recognize that the purpose prong carries a high evidentiary burden); *see also* sources cited *supra* note 3 (discussing recent evidence of laws enacted with the purpose of hindering a woman's choice to have an abortion).

[40] *Casey*, 505 U.S. at 887.

[41] *Id.* at 899. Since the effect of abortion restrictions on minors is an issue of great import, it requires its own separate analysis. Therefore, this article will focus only on restrictions in the general sense, and will not address the extra obstacles, concerns, and cases involving minors.

[42] *Id.* at 882. *See also infra* Part IV for a discussion on informed consent.

[43] *See id.* at 900-01.

[44] *Id.* at 895.

[45] *See* Borgmann, *supra* note 35, at 684-86 (discussing how the court applied the large fraction test to the husband notification provision and the concluding that the Court could have easily "defined the pool differently, to include those women for whom the requirement imposed burdens short of an insurmountable obstacle.").

other parts of their argument. Thus, the Court applied the standard in a modified way *in order to strike down the restriction.*[46]

Instead of a clear rule for lower courts to follow, the undue burden standard is one that can be shaped and molded in order to uphold or strike down a particular provision, according to the personal preferences of the Justices.[47] For instance, the *Casey* court dismissed the potential increase in the cost of an abortion *without* applying the large fraction test when it analyzed the waiting period provision.[48] The increase in cost for some women caused by the 24-hour waiting period was dismissed even though the District Court called it "particularly burdensome."[49] The plurality concluded that, "a particular burden is not of necessity a substantial obstacle. Whether a burden falls on a particular group is a distinct inquiry from whether it is a substantial obstacle even as to the women in that group. And the District Court did not conclude that the waiting period is such an obstacle even for the women who are most burdened by it."[50] Rather than remanding the case for a new ruling under the large fraction test, the plurality used the fact that the District Court failed to apply this test—a test the Court had not yet invented when the District Court decided *Casey*—as a reason to uphold the 24-hour waiting period.[51]

Had the *Casey* court applied the large fraction test in a manner similar to the way it applied the test to the husband notification

---

[46] *See* Wharton et al., *supra* note 30, at 333-35 (discussing the standard's application to the husband notification restriction).

[47] *See generally* Jeannie Suk, *Is Privacy a Woman?*, 97 Geo. L.J. 485 (2009) (discussing the Court's manipulation of the privacy standard, especially in the context of the large fraction test in *Casey*).

[48] For an excellent overview of how detrimental this portion of the *Casey* decision can be to rural women, depending on how lower courts apply the large fraction test and the undue burden standard, *see generally* Lisa R. Pruitt, *Toward a Feminist Theory of the Rural*, 2007 Utah L. Rev. 421, 463-483 (2007) (discussing how rural women have been both highlighted and ignored by courts and advocates in the context of abortion laws, and proposing hypothetical scenarios that illustrate the extreme hardship provisions like waiting periods and multiple trips may cause for rural women).

[49] *Casey*, 505 U.S. at 886.

[50] *Id.* at 887.

[51] *See* Martha A. Field, *Abortion Law Today*, 14 J. Legal Med. 3, 16 (1993) ("Indeed, it is not even certain precisely how the very statutory provisions at issue in Casey will fare under the undue burden test. Most of the requirements were upheld based explicitly on the factual findings entered by the district court .... [which] had not found a 'substantial burden' largely because that was not yet required and therefore the court was not looking for one."); *see also* Wharton et al., *supra* note 30, at 336 (applying a similar analysis of the logical inconsistencies of the *Casey* court's application of the large fraction test).

provision, the decision may have read, "it is common sense to as- sume that cost would apply as a restriction amounting to a sub- stantial obstacle for a large fraction of the women for whom cost is a concern."[52] However, the Court chose instead to apply the large fraction test as it saw fit—that is, only to the husband notification provision.[53] The Court did note that, "at some point increased cost could become a substantial obstacle,"[54] and so it is possible for fu- ture courts to use the malleability of the undue burden standard combined with the large fraction test in order to strike down such a restriction.[55]

It is worth noting that the plurality considered these restric- tions singly—not as a bundle. In no part of the opinion did the Court contemplate whether multiple restrictions could combine to create an undue burden on a woman's right to choose. This may be an unexplored area that could be challenged in future cases; how- ever, the *Casey* court's complete disregard of this reality suggests that the undue burden standard is not likely to be applied in this way.[56] Therefore, despite the onslaught of new restrictions enacted in the last decade,[57] the undue burden standard is not likely to be

---

[52] *See Casey*, 505 U.S. at 892 ("This information [about the spousal consent provision] and the District Court's finding reinforce what common sense would suggest."); *see also id.* at 894 ("The proper focus of constitutional inquiry is the group for whom the law is a restriction, not the group for whom the law is irrelevant."); *id.* at 895 ("[I]n a large fraction of the cases in which § 3209 is relevant, it will operate as a substantial obstacle to a woman's choice to undergo an abortion. It is an undue burden, and therefore invalid.").

[53] Although the Court seems to say that the standard is always applicable, stating, "[l]egislation is measured for consistency with the Constitution by its impact on those whose conduct it affects....[t]he proper focus of constitutional inquiry is the group for whom the law is a restriction, not the group for whom the law is irrelevant." *Casey*, 505 U.S. at 894. This is interesting language con- sidering that the Court did not openly apply the standard to any other provision at issue.

[54] *Id.* at 901.

[55] *See* Jill Hamers, Note, *Reeling in the Outlier: Gonzales v. Carhart and the End of Facial Challenges to Abortion Statutes*, 89 B.U. L. Rev. 1069, 1078-79 (2009) for a similar example of the logical inconsistency of the large fraction test. *See also Casey*, 505 U.S. at 926 (Blackmun, J., concurring in part and dis- senting in part) (anticipating that the Court would in fact use the standard to strike down restrictions rather than uphold them).

[56] *See* Wharton et al., *supra* note 30, at 322 n.24 (citing Dawn Johnsen, *The Outer Shell: The Hollowing Out of* Roe v. Wade, Slate, Jan. 25, 2006, http://www. slate.com/id/2134849).

[57] For a discussion of informed consent and fetal pain cases where "stacked" restrictions could be at issue in deciding constitutionality, *see infra* Parts III & IV. *See also* Borgmann, *supra* note 35, at 688-89 (discussing the Court's indiffer- ence to combined restrictions and the success of states in fashioning restrictions

applied to combined restrictions. Advocates, however, should continue to argue for its application in this way.

The next major use of the undue burden test was in the Supreme Court opinion striking down a Nebraska ban on so-called "partial birth abortions."[58] In *Stenberg v. Carhart*,[59] the Court said that not only was the ban too broad in that, "it imposes an undue burden on a woman's ability to choose a D & E abortion, thereby unduly burdening the right to choose abortion itself," but it also lacked a health exception[60] as required in both *Casey* and *Roe*.[61] The *Stenberg* court discussed extensively the different abortion procedures implicated in the ban and why doctors chose to perform them. Writing for the majority, Justice Breyer emphasized safety for the woman, but also said that Nebraska could have constructed the statute in such a way that would have permitted it to be upheld — that is, they could have constructed the statute so that it narrowly banned D & X (a type of abortion procedure similar in some respects to D & E), but included a health exception for the woman.[62]

So, while the health exception exclusion triggered invalidation under *Casey*, the majority also ruled that the statute was unconstitutional for a different reason. The Court again used the undue burden test to strike down the law on the basis that the language could be construed to include D & E procedures in the ban.[63] D & E is the most commonly used method for second trimester abortions, and therefore the Court deemed the outlawing of D & E procedures to be an undue burden on a woman's right to choose.[64] *Stenberg* was thus an interesting application of the undue burden test, in that the Court decided that the outlawing of a commonly

---

that cumulatively create substantial obstacles for women).

[58] Anti-choice activists have used this phrase to describe the dilation and extraction ("D & X") procedure, in which the doctor attempts to extract the fetus mostly intact, with as few passes of the doctor's instruments as possible (thereby eliminating various risks to the woman, *see* Stenberg v. Carhart, 530 U.S. 914, 932 (2000)), and where the fetal skull is crushed or brain contents evacuated before full extraction.

[59] *Stenberg*, 530 U.S. at 930 (citations and internal quotations omitted).

[60] *Id.*

[61] *See* Roe v. Wade, 410 U.S. 113, 164-65 (1973); Planned Parenthood of Se. Pa. v. Casey, 505 U.S. 833, 880 (1992).

[62] *See Stenberg*, 530 U.S. at 937-38.

[63] *Id.* at 943-46.

[64] *Id.* at 945-46.

used abortion procedure was enough to constitute a substantial obstacle to a woman's choice.

However, in a disappointing turn of events, *Stenberg* was effectively overruled seven years after it was decided.[65] In *Gonzales v. Carhart*, the Court upheld the Partial Birth Abortion Ban (PBAB) enacted by Congress in 2003. The PBAB banned D & X procedures, but despite *Stenberg* upholding the need for a health exception when banning any abortion procedure, the PBAB contained no such exception.[66] Moreover, the *Gonzales* court conclusively stated that the burden was on the challenger of the law to prove that it operated as hazardous to a large fraction of the women it affected.[67] Though an as-applied challenge is allowed,[68] it seems unrealistic to ask a woman to endure such a protracted court process, especially where abortion is concerned, in order to obtain a the procedure that would be best for her health.

The *Gonzales* majority emphasized that this procedure was not a necessary one because there were alternatives,[69] despite the fact that three separate district courts held that a D & X is safer for women in at least some circumstances,[70] and despite the fact that both the *Roe* and *Casey* courts required a health exception where necessary to preserve the health of the woman.[71] The Court also found that whether or not PBAB creates significant health risks for women is a "contested factual question."[72] Particularly disturbing is the following line from Kennedy's opinion:

> Considerations of marginal safety, including the balance of risks, are within the legislative competence when the regulation is rational and in pursuit of legitimate ends. When standard medical options are available, mere convenience does not suffice to displace them; and if some

---

[65] *See* Gonzales v. Carhart, 550 U.S. 124 (2007).

[66] *Id.* at 166-67.

[67] *Id.* at 167-68. Naturally, the women this provision affects are the women for whom a D & X procedure is medically recommended. Thus, the challenger would need to prove that a large fraction of these women would be at risk if they had to undergo a D & E (or some other procedure) in place of a D & X. Note that *Gonzales* departs from *Stenberg* in referring to the procedure as "intact D & E."

[68] *Id.* at 168.

[69] *Compare id.* at 164 *with Stenberg*, 530 U.S. at 937 ("The word 'necessary'...cannot refer to an absolute necessity or to absolute proof.").

[70] *Gonzales*, 550 U.S. at 162-63.

[71] *See* cases cited *supra* note 61.

[72] *Gonzales*, 550 U.S. at 161; *see also id.* at 162 ("There is documented medical disagreement whether the Act's prohibition would ever impose significant health risks on women.").

procedures have different risks than others, it does not follow that the State is altogether barred from imposing regulations.[73]

Here, Justice Kennedy delivers several blows to abortion rights. First, he leaves a woman's safety in the hands of legislators. While this might not seem to be a cause for concern, the *Roe, Casey,* and *Stenberg* courts gave much more constitutional protection to women's safety in the context of abortion regulations than many State governments.[74] Second, Justice Kennedy precluded the courts from interfering with abortion legislation in several circumstances. By giving State legislators an incredibly low standard (rationally related to legitimate ends), Justice Kennedy implicitly reduced the constitutionality standard to rational basis review for abortion legislation. Rational basis review is a relatively easy standard to survive. Under rational basis, as long as legislators can prove their abortion legislation is rationally related to legitimate ends, the courts must uphold it. However, some commentators assert that Justice Kennedy may only be applying rational basis with respect to the "purpose" prong of *Casey*.[75] That is, Kennedy may have only been referring to the government's reasoning for acting as it did.

This is not to say that the undue burden analysis is dead, because it is not. Kennedy does include it earlier in the opinion in conjunction with the rational basis language.[76] But where health-related regulations are concerned—and abortion regulations are health-related—this rational basis language may be revived. This

[73] *Id.* at 166.

[74] These cases gave more protection due to their inclusion of a health exception to abortion restrictions, where a woman is allowed to get an abortion even after the restricted period providing that her life or health is threatened. One of the more recent examples of State governments passing restrictions that threaten women's health are the so-called "wrongful birth" bills appearing in legislative dockets in more than half a dozen states in 2012. Kathy Lohr, *Should Parents be Able to Sue for 'Wrongful Birth?,'* NPR HEALTH BLOG (May 15, 2012, 3:01 AM), http://www.npr.org/blogs/health/2012/05/15/152687638/should-parents-be-able-to-sue-for-wrongful-birth. These bills would ostensibly allow doctors to withhold information about fetal abnormalities from their patients in order to prevent abortions. *Id.* Legislators working on the bills are very open about the fact that they are "pro-life" measures, and yet the health and life of the women involved is effectively ignored.

[75] *See* Jessie Hill, *The Constitutional Right to Make Medical Treatment Decisions: A Tale of Two Doctrines,* 86 TEX. L. REV. 277, 320-21 (2007).

[76] *Gonzales,* 550 U.S. at 158 ("Where it has a rational basis to act, and it does not impose an undue burden, the State may use its regulatory power to bar certain procedures and substitute others, all in furtherance of its legitimate interests in regulating the medical profession in order to promote respect for life, including life of the unborn.").

again seems like an instance of the Court modifying the standard, or supplementing it with other tests, in order to uphold what they want to uphold.[77]

Moreover, Kennedy classifies the entire decision as a consideration of "marginal safety."[78] As the *Stenberg* opinion notes,[79] the considerations here are not marginal. Though D & E is a safe procedure, when physicians are not allowed to choose the safest procedure for each individual case, the health implications for women are potentially serious.[80] Justice Kennedy's dismissive treatment of these health risks, evidenced not only by his "marginal safety" language, but also by his indication that this is an issue of mere "convenience,"[81] is highly troubling. Though there is no evidence of lower federal courts using this particular part of the *Gonzales* opinion, it has only been five years, and with the current climate surrounding abortion regulations[82] there is reason to fear it may become part of future decisions.

Nevertheless, even if the language from *Gonzales* has not yet affected the way the courts treat abortion restrictions, the case as a whole has certainly emboldened the legislature to enact more restrictive laws around abortion. In 2007, Professor Jack Balkin said,

> [*Gonzales*] might lead states to pass a wide range of new laws under the rubric of "informed consent" that would require doctors to show women the results of ultrasound imaging of the fetus before it is aborted, to describe in gruesome detail how the fetus will be terminated, dismembered and removed, to offer the state's views on the existence of any pain the fetus might feel when it

---

[77] *See* earlier discussion on the husband notification provision, *supra*, where the court creates the "large fraction test" and uses it only on this provision, ostensibly in order to strike it down.

[78] *Gonzales*, 550 U.S. at 166.

[79] *See* Stenberg v. Carhart, 530 U.S. 914, 932-36 (2000) (summarizing medical evidence supporting the Court's finding that the health benefits of a D & X procedure outweigh any potential risks).

[80] *See id.* at 929 (recounting Dr. Carhart's testimony in front of the District Court regarding the variety of circumstances under which a ban on the D & X procedure may have particularly dangerous consequences).

[81] *Gonzales*, 550 U.S. at 166.

[82] *See States Enact a Record Number of Abortion Restrictions in First Half of 2011*, GUTTMACHER INST. (July 13, 2011), http://www.guttmacher.org/media/inthenews/2011/07/13/index.html.

is destroyed; and, in general, ratchet up the emotional anxiety of women who are about to undergo abortions.[83]

As the article demonstrates in Part IV, many of these fears have come to pass.[84]

Lastly, this opinion led the Supreme Court to wade deeper into the morass of morals surrounding abortion politics. Justice Kennedy highlights that the Court is allowed to draw boundaries, "to prevent certain practices that extinguish life and are close to actions that are condemned."[85] If viewed broadly, this could be interpreted as Kennedy indicating that the Court can proscribe abortion completely, since there are many anti-choice activists who conceive of abortion as "close to" murder (while many of them believe it *is* murder[86]). Therefore, from this language, it seems that the Court is giving itself free reign to further restrict access to abortion.

Thus, the undue burden test as applied by the Supreme Court is still a relatively unclear one. Using the husband notification provision and PBAB as clear contrasting examples of its application, the test seems to hinge on Justices' subjective preferences, with the Court supplementing the standard with other tests (large fraction and rational basis) when necessary. This provides muddled guidance to lower courts. Federal courts have been divided in their application of the standard, even when focusing on one particular aspect of regulations.[87]

Therefore, the undue burden standard should be clarified and strengthened, especially regarding the propensity for the accumulation of multiple abortion restrictions to create a substantial obstacle.[88] To do this, advocates should urge courts to analyze whether or not multiple restrictions at once would be an undue burden for a large fraction of the women to whom those multiple restrictions

---

[83] Jack Balkin, *The Big News About* Gonzales v. Carhart—*It's the Informed Consent, Stupid*, BALKINIZATION (Apr. 19, 2007, 2:50 PM), http://balkin.blogspot.com/2007/04/big-news-about-gonzales-v-carhart.html.

[84] *See infra* Part IV.

[85] *Gonzales*, 550 U.S. at 158.

[86] As an example, typing in "abortion is murder" into Google.com gets 2,010,000 hits as of May 17, 2012. On the first page, six of the ten hits are anti-choice ("pro-life") websites. Three are critiques of the anti-choice "abortion is murder" stance. On Youtube.com, the same phrase gets approximately 5,460 hits. All of the videos on the first page (twenty-two) are anti-choice testimonies about why abortion is murder.

[87] *See infra* Part IV (discussing the divided application of the undue burden standard to informed consent provisions).

[88] *See* Borgmann, *supra* note 35, at 688-89 (discussing the Court's indifference to combined restrictions, and the success of states in fashioning restrictions that cumulatively create substantial obstacles for women).

apply. Further, the "purpose" prong of the undue burden standard should not be ignored,[89] in light of evidence that legislatures are passing laws with the clear purpose[90] of preventing women from obtaining abortions.[91] This is in line with *Casey's* declaration that, "the means chosen by the State to further the interest in potential

---

[89] *See supra* note 3.

[90] While many news outlets and commentators within the last few years (and beyond) include abortion restrictions under the banner of a "war on women," the clearest example of this in the abortion context happened in Mississippi in May 2012. Mississippi governor Phil Bryant signed a law, H.B. 1390, that requires anyone who performs an abortion to be a licensed obstetrician-gynecologist with admitting privileges at a local hospital. H.B. 1390, Reg. Sess. (Miss. 2012), 2012, available at http://billstatus.ls.state.ms.us/documents/2012/pdf/HB/1300-1399/HB1390SG.pdf. Upon signing the law, Bryant said, "Today you see the first step in a movement, I believe, to do what we campaigned on—to say we're going to try to end abortion in Mississippi." Emily Wagner Pettus, *Miss. Gov. Signs New Limits on Abortion Providers*, NECN.com (April 16, 2012, 12:06 PM), http://www.necn.com/04/16/12/Miss-gov-signing-new-abortion-regulation/landing.html?&apID=7b1c71f1fb8e4d5b95a235234518002f. About one month later, a representative instrumental in the bill's passage said the following,

> We have literally stopped abortion in the state of Mississippi. Three blocks from the Capitol sits the only abortion clinic in the state of Mississippi. A bill was drafted. It said, if you would perform an abortion in the state of Mississippi, you must be a certified OB/GYN and you must have admitting privileges to a hospital. Anybody here in the medical field knows how hard it is to get admitting privileges to a hospital....It's going to be challenged, of course, in the Supreme Court and all—but literally, we stopped abortion in the state of Mississippi, legally, without having to— *Roe vs. Wade.* So we've done that. I was proud of it. The governor signed it into law. And of course, there you have the other side. They're like, "Well, the poor pitiful women that can't afford to go out of state are just going to start doing them at home with a coat hanger." That's what we've heard over and over and over. But hey, you have to have moral values. You have to start somewhere, and that's what we've decided to do. This became law and the governor signed it, and I think for one time, we were first in the nation in the state of Mississippi.

Kirsten West Sivali, *Mississippi Rep on Abortion Being Illegal: "Let Women Use Coat Hangers,"* NEWSONE (May 15, 2012), http://newsone.com/2015625/illegal-abortion-mississippi/.

[91] *But see* Harper Jean Tobin, *Confronting Misinformation on Abortion: Informed Consent, Deference, and Fetal Pain Laws*, 17 COLUM. J. GENDER & L. 111, 126 n.85 (2008) (explaining that it is not easy to determine where the Court will fall on legislative purpose inquiries, which are often "vexing" and "controversial.").

life must be calculated to inform the woman's free choice, not hinder it."[92]

IV. INFORMED CONSENT

Though many types of abortion restrictions exist in state law,[93] one of the most widely used, after parental consent and waiting periods, is the informed consent provision first upheld in *Casey*.[94] The basic concept behind informed consent restrictions is that, to protect the woman and the potential life she carries, the woman should be as informed as possible about the procedure and about alternative options to an abortion.[95] Though regulations vary as to how much and about what the woman should be informed, fetal pain laws and pre-abortion ultrasounds are the most commonly found informed consent provisions in abortion legislation.[96]

Informed consent was first used in the verbal explanation of the nature of the procedure, risks/alternatives, the gestational age

---

[92] *See Casey*, 505 U.S. at 822. *See also* Tobin, *supra* note 91, at 126 (explaining that this elucidation of the purpose prong is in line with a rational basis review standard as articulated by the Eighth Circuit when it said, "[w]here a requirement serves no purpose other than to make abortions more difficult, it strikes at the heart of a protected right, and is an unconstitutional burden on that right." (quoting Planned Parenthood of Greater Iowa, Inc. v. Atchison, 126 F.3d 1042, 1049 (8th Cir. 1997)) (emphasis omitted)).

[93] *See State Policies in Brief: An Overview of Abortion Laws*, GUTTMACHER INST. (Oct. 1, 2012), http://www.guttmacher.org/statecenter/spibs/spib_OAL.pdf [hereinafter *Overview of Abortion Laws*].

[94] *See* Planned Parenthood of Se. Pa. v. Casey, 505 U.S. 833, 882 (1992). *See also id.* at 872 ("Though the woman has a right to choose to terminate or continue her pregnancy before viability, it does not at all follow that the State is prohibited from taking steps to ensure that this choice is thoughtful and informed. Even in the earliest stages of pregnancy, the State may enact rules and regulations designed to encourage her to know that there are philosophic and social arguments of great weight that can be brought to bear in favor of continuing the pregnancy to full term and that there are procedures and institutions to allow adoption of unwanted children as well as a certain degree of state assistance if the mother chooses to raise the child herself."). The Court then quotes Webster v. Reprod. Health Servs., 492 U.S. 490, 511 (1989) in saying that it is constitutional for a state to express a preference for childbirth over abortion.

[95] *Id.* at 877. This differs from the basic medical definition of informed consent, which refers to medical alternatives rather than non-medical alternatives to a medical procedure.

[96] *See* Overview of Abortion Laws *supra* note 93 (five states require information on the scientifically disputed link between abortion and breast cancer, eight states require information on the potential long-term mental health consequences of an abortion, and eleven states require information about fetal

of the fetus, the existence of pamphlets bearing further information, the state assistance available to her in carrying her child to term, and the father's obligations.[97] More recently, informed consent has been used to justify mandatory ultrasounds and pamphlets about "fetal pain."[98]

It is important to note that informed consent in the abortion context is different from informed consent as it is used in other medical contexts. The difference exposes informed consent provisions as patronizing laws[99] that treat women who choose to abort as

---

pain. Further, twelve states require information on the availability of an ultrasound. *See State Policies in Brief: Requirements for Ultrasound*, GUTTMACHER INST. (Oct. 1, 2012), http://www.guttmacher.org/statecenter/spibs/spib_RFU.pdf [hereinafter *Requirements for Ultrasound*]. This is separate from the twenty-one states that regulate ultrasounds in one of the four ways mentioned in section IV(A), *infra*, though all ultrasound requirements are grouped under "informed consent," since that is their ultimate stated purpose. *See id.*

[97] *See Casey*, 505 U.S. at 902-903 (appendix to majority opinion).

[98] *See infra* Part IV(B) on fetal pain legislation.

[99] Consider the following text from the Wisconsin Statute on Voluntary and Informed Consent for Abortions:

(1) Legislative findings and intent. (a) The legislature finds that:

1. Many women now seek or are encouraged to undergo elective abortions without full knowledge of the medical and psychological risks of abortion, development of the unborn child or of alternatives to abortion. An abortion decision is often made under stressful circumstances.

2. The knowledgeable exercise of a woman's decision to have an elective abortion depends on the extent to which the woman receives sufficient information to make a voluntary and informed choice between 2 alternatives of great consequence: carrying a child to birth or undergoing an abortion.

3. The U.S. supreme court has stated: "In attempting to ensure that a woman apprehend the full consequences of her decision, the State furthers the legitimate purpose of reducing the risk that a woman may elect an abortion, only to discover later, with devastating psychological consequences, that her decision was not fully informed." Planned Parenthood of Southeastern Pennsylvania v. Casey, 112 U.S. 2791, 2823 (1992).

4. It is essential to the psychological and physical well-being of a woman considering an elective abortion that she receive complete and accurate information on all options available to her in dealing with her pregnancy.

5. The vast majority of elective abortions in this state are performed in clinics that are devoted solely to providing abortions and family planning services. Women who seek elective abortions at these facilities normally do not have a prior patient-physician relationship with the physician who is to perform or induce the abortion, normally do not return to the facility for post-operative care and normally do not continue a patient-physician relation-

ship with the physician who performed or induced the abortion. In most instances, the woman's only actual contact with the physician occurs simultaneously with the abortion procedure, with little opportunity to receive personal counseling by the physician concerning her decision. Because of this, certain safeguards are necessary to protect a woman's right to know.

6. A reasonable waiting period is critical to ensure that a woman has the fullest opportunity to give her voluntary and informed consent before she elects to undergo an abortion.

(b) It is the intent of the legislature in enacting this section to further the important and compelling state interests in all of the following:

1. Protecting the life and health of the woman subject to an elective abortion and, to the extent constitutionally permissible, the life of her unborn child.

2. Fostering the development of standards of professional conduct in the practice of abortion.

3. Ensuring that prior to the performance or inducement of an elective abortion, the woman considering an elective abortion receive personal counseling by the physician and be given a full range of information regarding her pregnancy, her unborn child, the abortion, the medical and psychological risks of abortion and available alternatives to the abortion.

4. Ensuring that a woman who decides to have an elective abortion gives her voluntary and informed consent to the abortion procedure.

Wis. Stat. Ann. § 253.10(1) (West 2012), *amended* by 2011 Wis. Legis. Serv. 217 (West).

It is routine for state legislatures to frame these acts as a "woman's right." In fact, in many instances the act itself is named something along the lines of "A Woman's Right to Know Act." The language used in the acts comes right out and says that women often seek or are "encouraged" to seek abortions without knowing the full "medical and emotional" consequences of their decision, implying that women do not really know what the outcome of an abortion might be. Having worked on a hotline about options for unplanned pregnancy, I can say with confidence that many women agonize over the decision of whether or not to terminate. While unplanned pregnancy is certainly stressful, it is reminiscent of the "hysteria" argument to imply that women cannot make rational and informed decisions under stress. *See* Reva B. Siegel, *The New Politics of Abortion: An Equality Analysis of Woman-Protective Abortion Restrictions*, 2007 U. Ill. L. Rev. 991, 1033 n.169 (2007) (citing early antiabortion arguments that appealed to the notion of women as hysterical). Moreover, the framing of the argument in the statute above does not support its conclusions, but rather simply states them as though they are undisputed facts. This is especially true regarding the waiting period provision, § 253.10 (1)(a)(6). This is why I and other commentators characterize these statutes as patronizing. *Cf.* Reva B. Siegel, *Dignity and the Politics of Protection: Abortion Restrictions Under Casey/Carhart*, 117 Yale L.J. 1694, 1715 (2008) (discussing what Siegel dubs the "woman-protective antiabortion argument (WPAA), a political discourse that taps longstanding traditions of gender paternalism and is designed to persuade voters who ambivalently support abortion rights that they can help women by

less capable of understanding the potential outcomes than patients in other medical contexts.[100]

Originally formulated in common law, informed consent is largely related to notions of bodily autonomy and self-determination, and its first articulation is widely attributed to Justice Cardozo's *Schloendorff v. Society of New York Hospitals* opinion: "Every human being of adult years and sound mind has a right to determine what shall be done with his own body; and a surgeon who performs an operation without his patient's consent commits assault."[101] As articulated in a later decision, informed consent must be tempered by medical discretion, and with concern for the patient's emotional wellbeing.[102] However, commentators and courts also note that to be truly informed, patients must be aware of the risks, benefits, and alternatives to a procedure.[103] Therefore, it would seem that under the traditional definition of informed consent, risks, benefits, and alternatives could be communicated at the discretion of the physician, which would include the physician's estimation of the balance between necessary information and unnecessary information that would be harmful to the patient's emotional state.

However, in abortion jurisprudence, despite earlier decisions that largely adhered to the traditional medical informed consent standard discussed above,[104] *Casey* and post-*Casey* decisions on abortion have formulated a different sort of informed consent standard premised on the state's interest in preserving life. In fact, *Casey* notes that it is explicitly departing from precedent by allowing the state to mandate informed consent provisions even when these provisions are clearly biased against abortion.[105] In discussing previous cases, the *Casey* court declared that to the extent that those cases held unconstitutional "truthful, nonmisleading information about the nature of the procedure, the attendant health risks and those of childbirth, and the 'probable gestational age' of the fetus,

---

using law to restrict women's access to abortion.").

[100] *See* Manian, *supra* note 34, at 235.

[101] *Id.* (quoting Schloendorff v. Soc'y of N.Y. Hosp., 105 N.E. 92, 93 (1914)).

[102] *See* Salgo v. Leland Stanford Jr. Univ. Bd. of Trs., 317 P.2d 170, 181 (Cal. Ct. App. 1957).

[103] *See* Manian, *supra* note 34, at 237. For a thorough breakdown of the history of Court decisions about informed consent, *see id.* at 236-239.

[104] *See id.* at 244-46. The 1986 Supreme Court even took the state to task for imposing its views on a woman and inserting itself into the physician-woman dialogue under the guise of an informed consent provision. See *id.* at 246, n. 148 (citing Thornburgh v. Am. Coll. of Obstetricians & Gynecologists, 476 U.S. 747, 762-63 (1986)).

[105] *See* Manian, *supra* note 34, at 250.

those cases go too far, are inconsistent with *Roe*'s acknowledgment of an important interest in potential life, and are overruled."[106] The Court goes on to say,

> It cannot be questioned that psychological well-being is a facet of health. Nor can it be doubted that most women considering an abortion would deem the impact on the fetus relevant, if not dispositive, to the decision. In attempting to ensure that a woman apprehend the full consequences of her decision, the State furthers the legitimate purpose of reducing the risk that a woman may elect an abortion, only to discover later, with devastating psychological consequences, that her decision was not fully informed. If the information the State requires to be made available to the woman is truthful and not misleading, the requirement may be permissible.[107]

Therefore, these laws are ostensibly both designed and justified by the Court under the premise that an ill-considered choice to terminate a pregnancy can cause psychological damage to a woman.[108] These restrictions are also upheld under the premise that they protect the state's interest in potential life since, theoretically, some women may choose not to have an abortion after being informed more fully about the "consequences" of the procedure.[109] The standard, then, is that states may enact restrictions that are designed to ensure that "so grave a choice is well informed,"[110] so long as these restrictions are "truthful, and not misleading."[111]

The next section analyzes how federal courts are treating informed consent provisions, with a focus on the two most common informed consent provisions—pre-abortion ultrasounds and information concerning fetal pain. Ostensibly because challenges under the undue burden standard would not be legally sufficient to enjoin these specific informed consent provisions, activists have recently begun challenging some informed consent laws under First Amendment compelled speech precedent—sometimes including an undue

---

[106] Planned Parenthood of Se. Pa. v. Casey, 505 U.S. 833, 882 (1992).

[107] *Id.*

[108] *See* Gonzales v. Carhart, 550 U.S. 124, 159-160 (2007) for Kennedy's extensive litany on the potential of psychological pain due to lack of knowledge about the abortion procedure; *see also* Siegel, *Dignity and the Politics of Protection: Abortion Restrictions Under* Casey/Carhart, *supra* note 99, at 1715.

[109] *Casey*, 505 U.S. at 873.

[110] *Gonzales*, 550 U.S. at 159.

[111] *Casey*, 505 U.S. at 882.

burden argument and sometimes not.[112] This tactic, while a creative use of advocacy, should also be combined with challenges under the undue burden standard, with an emphasis on the purpose prong and a more consistent application of the large fraction test.

A. *Ultrasound Laws*

Ultrasound-focused informed consent laws can be grouped into four categories.[113] Group A legislation does not require the provider to perform an ultrasound, but it gives women the option to have an ultrasound and subsequently view an ultrasound image,[114] In Group B legislation, the provider is mandated to perform an ultrasound and offer the woman a chance to view the ultrasound.[115] Group C legislation mandates an ultrasound and then requires the physician to display the ultrasound image on a screen where the patient can see it (though she has the option of whether or not to look at it).[116] Group D legislation is similar to Group C with the added proviso that the provider must describe aloud what he or she

---

[112] *E.g.*, Stuart v. Huff, 834 F. Supp. 2d 424 (M.D.N.C. 2011); Tex. Med. Providers Performing Abortion Servs. v. Lakey, 667 F.3d 570 (5th Cir. 2012); Planned Parenthood of the Heartland v. Heineman, 724 F. Supp. 2d 1025 (D. Neb. 2010); Eubanks v. Schmidt, 126 F. Supp. 2d 451 (W.D. Ky. 2000).

[113] I first encountered the breakdown of ultrasound laws into three groups in Godzeno's article, *supra* note 11, at 303-21. Godzeno's analysis adds clarity to a confusing set of restrictions. As such, I utilize his breakdown here with the addition of Group D legislation.

[114] *Id.* at 305.

[115] *Id.* at 310.

[116] *See id.* at 316-17 (for our purposes, I am breaking up Godzeno's Group C into two separate groups).

sees on the ultrasound screen.[117] These are typically referred to as

[117] See the following text from Texas's voluntary and informed consent statute:

(a) Consent to an abortion is voluntary and informed only if:

(1) the physician who is to perform the abortion informs the pregnant woman on whom the abortion is to be performed of:

(A) the physician's name;

(B) the particular medical risks associated with the particular abortion procedure to be employed, including, when medically accurate:

(i) the risks of infection and hemorrhage;

(ii) the potential danger to a subsequent pregnancy and of infertility; and

(iii) the possibility of increased risk of breast cancer following an induced abortion and the natural protective effect of a completed pregnancy in avoiding breast cancer;

(C) the probable gestational age of the unborn child at the time the abortion is to be performed; and

(D) the medical risks associated with carrying the child to term;

(2) the physician who is to perform the abortion or the physician's agent informs the pregnant woman that:

(A) medical assistance benefits may be available for prenatal care, childbirth, and neonatal care;

(B) the father is liable for assistance in the support of the child without regard to whether the father has offered to pay for the abortion; and

(C) public and private agencies provide pregnancy prevention counseling and medical referrals for obtaining pregnancy prevention medications or devices, including emergency contraception for victims of rape or incest;

(3) the physician who is to perform the abortion or the physician's agent:

(A) provides the pregnant woman with the printed materials described by Section 171.014; and

(B) informs the pregnant woman that those materials:

(i) have been provided by the Department of State Health Services;

(ii) are accessible on an Internet website sponsored by the department;

(iii) describe the unborn child and list agencies that offer alternatives to abortion; and

(iv) include a list of agencies that offer sonogram services at no cost to the pregnant woman;

(4) before any sedative or anesthesia is administered to the pregnant woman and at least 24 hours before the abortion or at least two hours before the abortion if the pregnant woman waives this requirement by certifying that she currently lives 100 miles or more from the nearest abortion provider that is a facility licensed under Chapter 245 or a facility that performs more than 50 abortions in any 12-month period:

(A) the physician who is to perform the abortion or an agent of the physician who is also a sonographer certified by a national registry of medical sonographers performs a sonogram on the pregnant woman on whom the abortion is to be performed;

(B) the physician who is to perform the abortion displays the sonogram images in a quality consistent with current medical practice in a manner that the pregnant woman may view them;

(C) the physician who is to perform the abortion provides, in a manner understandable to a layperson, a verbal explanation of the results of the sonogram images, including a medical description of the dimensions of the embryo or fetus, the presence of cardiac activity, and the presence of external members and internal organs; and

(D) the physician who is to perform the abortion or an agent of the physician who is also a sonographer certified by a national registry of medical sonographers makes audible the heart auscultation for the pregnant woman to hear, if present, in a quality consistent with current medical practice and provides, in a manner understandable to a layperson, a simultaneous verbal explanation of the heart auscultation;

(5) before receiving a sonogram under Subdivision (4)(A) and before the abortion is performed and before any sedative or anesthesia is administered, the pregnant woman completes and certifies with her signature an election form that states as follows:

"ABORTION AND SONOGRAM ELECTION

(1) THE INFORMATION AND PRINTED MATERIALS DESCRIBED BY SECTIONS 171.012(A)(1)-(3), TEXAS HEALTH AND SAFETY CODE, HAVE BEEN PROVIDED AND EXPLAINED TO ME.

(2) I UNDERSTAND THE NATURE AND CONSEQUENCES OF AN ABORTION.

(3) TEXAS LAW REQUIRES THAT I RECEIVE A SONOGRAM PRIOR TO RECEIVING AN ABORTION.

(4) I UNDERSTAND THAT I HAVE THE OPTION TO VIEW THE SONOGRAM IMAGES.

(5) I UNDERSTAND THAT I HAVE THE OPTION TO HEAR THE HEARTBEAT.

(6) I UNDERSTAND THAT I AM REQUIRED BY LAW TO HEAR AN EXPLANATION OF THE SONOGRAM IMAGES UNLESS I CERTIFY IN WRITING TO ONE OF THE FOLLOWING:

_____ I AM PREGNANT AS A RESULT OF A SEXUAL ASSAULT, INCEST, OR OTHER VIOLATION OF THE TEXAS PENAL CODE THAT HAS BEEN REPORTED TO LAW ENFORCEMENT AUTHORITIES OR THAT HAS NOT BEEN REPORTED BECAUSE I REASONABLY BELIEVE THAT DOING SO WOULD PUT ME AT RISK OF RETALIATION RESULTING IN SERIOUS BODILY INJURY.

_____ I AM A MINOR AND OBTAINING AN ABORTION IN ACCORDANCE WITH JUDICIAL BYPASS PROCEDURES UNDER CHAPTER 33, TEXAS FAMILY CODE.

_____ MY FETUS HAS AN IRREVERSIBLE MEDICAL CONDITION OR ABNORMALITY, AS IDENTIFIED BY RELIABLE DIAGNOSTIC PROCEDURES AND DOCUMENTED IN MY MEDICAL FILE.

(7) I AM MAKING THIS ELECTION OF MY OWN FREE WILL AND WITHOUT COERCION.

(8) FOR A WOMAN WHO LIVES 100 MILES OR MORE FROM THE NEAREST ABORTION PROVIDER THAT IS A FACILITY LICENSED UNDER CHAPTER 245 OR A FACILITY THAT PERFORMS MORE THAN 50 ABORTIONS IN ANY 12-MONTH PERIOD ONLY:

I CERTIFY THAT, BECAUSE I CURRENTLY LIVE 100 MILES OR MORE FROM THE NEAREST ABORTION PROVIDER THAT IS A FACILITY LICENSED UNDER CHAPTER 245 OR A FACILITY THAT PERFORMS MORE THAN 50 ABORTIONS IN ANY 12-MONTH PERIOD, I WAIVE THE REQUIREMENT TO WAIT 24 HOURS AFTER THE SONOGRAM IS PERFORMED BEFORE RECEIVING THE ABORTION PROCEDURE. MY PLACE OF RESIDENCE IS: _____.

_____ | _____

SIGNATURE   DATE

(6) before the abortion is performed, the physician who is to perform the abortion receives a copy of the signed, written certification required by Subdivision (5); and

(7) the pregnant woman is provided the name of each person who provides or explains the information required under this subsection .

(a-1) During a visit made to a facility to fulfill the requirements of Subsection (a), the facility and any person at the facility may not accept any form of payment, deposit, or exchange or make any financial agreement for an abortion or abortion-related services other than for payment of a service required by Subsection (a). The amount charged for a service required by Subsection (a) may not exceed the reimbursement rate established for the service by the Health and Human Services Commission for statewide medical reimbursement programs.

(b) The information required to be provided under Subsections (a)(1) and (2) may not be provided by audio or video recording and must be provided at least 24 hours before the abortion is to be performed:

(1) orally and in person in a private and confidential setting if the pregnant woman currently lives less than 100 miles from the nearest abortion provider that is a facility licensed under Chapter 245 or a facility that performs more than 50 abortions in any 12-month period; or

(2) orally by telephone or in person in a private and confidential setting if the pregnant woman certifies that the woman currently lives 100 miles or more from the nearest abortion provider that

"speech and display" requirements.[118]

Pro-choice groups argue that since ultrasounds are not typically medically necessary, these ultrasound requirements are government attempts to "personify the fetus and dissuade a woman from obtaining an abortion."[119] There are no reliable statistics as to whether this tactic actually works, but "[a]necdotal evidence from abortion providers suggests mandated disclosures have little if any effect on women's ultimate decisions."[120] In fact, many women have serious misconceptions about potential consequences from abortion and still elect the procedure.[121] This is not surprising

---

is a facility licensed under Chapter 245 or a facility that performs more than 50 abortions in any 12-month period .

(c) When providing the information under Subsection (a)(3) , the physician or the physician's agent must provide the pregnant woman with the address of the Internet website on which the printed materials described by Section 171.014 may be viewed as required by Section 171.014(e).

(d) The information provided to the woman under Subsection (a)(2)(B) must include, based on information available from the Office of the Attorney General and the United States Department of Health and Human Services Office of Child Support Enforcement for the three-year period preceding the publication of the information, information regarding the statistical likelihood of collecting child support.

(e) The department is not required to republish informational materials described by Subsection (a)(2)(B) because of a change in information described by Subsection (d) unless the statistical information in the materials changes by five percent or more.

TEX. HEALTH & SAFETY CODE ANN. § 171.012(a) - § 171.012(e) (West 2012). This statute, in Texas, was the only so-called "speech and display" statute to be upheld by a Circuit Court. *See Lakey*, 667 F.3d at 584; Scott W. Gaylord & Thomas J. Molony, Casey *and a Woman's Right to Know: Ultrasounds, Informed Consent, and the First Amendment* 1 (Elon Univ. Sch. of Law, Working Paper No. 2012-02, 2012), *available at* http://ssrn.com/abstract=2017041. Note: This article will not be exploring the *type* of ultrasound required by law. Recently, three states (Texas, Oklahoma, and Virginia) have attempted to pass legislation that requires a transvaginal ultrasound rather than the more common abdominal ultrasound. This type of ultrasound is normally used by physicians prior to eight weeks of pregnancy or when there is a specific issue that needs more clarity, as some doctors feel it is easier to see when a transvaginal ultrasound is used. Pro-choice activists have come out against transvaginal ultrasounds, noting implications for survivors of assault (though ostensibly women may opt out if they say they have been assaulted).

[118] Gaylord & Molony, *supra* note 117, at 3.

[119] Requirements for Ultrasound, *supra* note 96.

[120] Tobin, *supra* note 91, at 124.

[121] *Id*. at 125.

considering the pre-*Roe* evidence of women braving highly dangerous conditions to obtain an abortion.[122]

Informed consent provisions in general have been challenged
many times and some of these cases also involved First Amendment challenges to physician speech.[123] The courts differ in their
manner of addressing First Amendment challenges in the context
of abortion regulations, leaving a split in the Circuits on how to
address informed consent provisions. Only one recent case about
informed consent procedures has utilized the undue burden standard—and even then, the standard was not fully analyzed.[124]

1. The Ultrasound Cases

The first case to address ultrasound requirements was *Karlin v. Foust* in 1996.[125] In *Karlin*, plaintiffs challenged Wisconsin's
abortion informed consent statute on three grounds: (1) certain
provisions were unconstitutionally vague; (2) the statute violated
the Due Process Clause of the Fourteenth Amendment because
it imposed an "undue burden" on a woman's right to an abortion;
and (3) two First Amendment challenges.[126] Specifically, the plaintiffs argued that the provision requiring the physician to inform the
patient that fetal auscultation[127] and imaging services (via ultrasound) were available[128] imposed an undue burden on a woman's

---

[122] *Id.*

[123] *See supra* note 112.

[124] Tex. Med. Providers Performing Abortion Servs. v. Lakey, 667 F.3d 570,
574-77 (5th Cir. 2012) (see Part IV(A)(1), *infra*, for a full discussion of the
Lakey court's use of the undue burden standard).

[125] Karlin v. Foust, 975 F. Supp 1177 (W.D.Wisc. 1997).

[126] *Id.* at 1201. The District Court dismissed the First Amendment challenges
simply by noting that, "The Supreme Court resolved that First Amendment
question against physicians in *Casey* and it cannot be reopened here." *Id.* at
1226.

[127] Auscultation is medical terminology that refers to listening to sounds
within the body—specifically, the heart, lungs, and blood. *See Auscultation*,
HOWARD HUGHES MED. INST., http://www.hhmi.org/biointeractive/vlabs/cardiol-
ogy/content/dtg/ausc/ausc.html (last visited Oct. 28, 2012) (defining auscultation and demonstrating different types of aortic phenomena with sound files).
Here, it specifically refers to the fetal heartbeat. *See Karlin*, 975 F. Supp. at
1218-19.

[128] See the following portion of the text of the Wisconsin statute, including
the requirement in § 253.10(3)(c)(1)(g) that a fetal ultrasound be available.

(3)(c) *Informed consent*. Except if a medical emergency exists,
a woman›s consent to an abortion is informed only if all of the
following first take place:
1. Except as provided in sub. (3m), at least 24 hours before the

abortion is to be performed or induced, the physician who is to perform or induce the abortion or any other qualified physician has, in person, orally informed the woman of all of the following:

a. Whether or not, according to the reasonable medical judgment of the physician, the woman is pregnant.

b. The probable gestational age of the unborn child at the time that the information is provided. The physician or other qualified physician shall also provide this information to the woman in writing at this time.

c. The particular medical risks, if any, associated with the woman's pregnancy.

d. The probable anatomical and physiological characteristics of the woman's unborn child at the time the information is given.

e. The details of the medical or surgical method that would be used in performing or inducing the abortion.

f. The medical risks associated with the particular abortion procedure that would be used, including the risks of infection, psychological trauma, hemorrhage, endometritis, perforated uterus, incomplete abortion, failed abortion, danger to subsequent pregnancies and infertility.

g. That fetal ultrasound imaging and auscultation of fetal heart tone services are available that enable a pregnant woman to view the image or hear the heartbeat of her unborn child. In so informing the woman and describing these services, the physician shall advise the woman as to how she may obtain these services if she desires to do so.

h. The recommended general medical instructions for the woman to follow after an abortion to enhance her safe recovery and the name and telephone number of a physician to call if complications arise after the abortion.

hm. If the abortion is induced by an abortion-inducing drug, that the woman must return to the abortion facility for a follow-up visit 12 to 18 days after the use of an abortion-inducing drug to confirm the termination of the pregnancy and evaluate the woman's medical condition.

i. If, in the reasonable medical judgment of the physician, the woman's unborn child has reached viability, that the physician who is to perform or induce the abortion is required to take all steps necessary under s. 940.15 to preserve and maintain the life and health of the child.

j. Any other information that a reasonable patient would consider material and relevant to a decision of whether or not to carry a child to birth or to undergo an abortion.

jm. That the woman has a right to refuse to consent to an abortion, that her consent is not voluntary if anyone is coercing her to consent to an abortion against her will, and that it is unlawful for the physician to perform or induce the abortion without her voluntary consent.

k. That the woman may withdraw her consent to have an abortion at any time before the abortion is performed or induced.

right to an abortion because it violated *Casey's* "truthful and not misleading" requirement.[129] The District Court found the plaintiffs' argument persuasive and reasoned that because a fetal heartbeat was not actually available until at least the twelfth week of pregnancy, requiring a physician to tell the patient that certain procedures were available when they were not, would be "an unconstitutional undue burden on a woman's right to choose."[130] Nevertheless, the District Court chose to sever this provision (and others it found to be unconstitutional) from the statute, while maintaining the rest of the law.[131]

On appeal, plaintiffs argued that the informed consent provision was unconstitutionally vague, which would have a chilling effect on physicians' willingness to perform abortions, thus imposing an undue burden on a woman's right to choose.[132] The Court of Appeals for the Seventh Circuit dismissed plaintiffs' vagueness challenge.[133] The court found that the law was not vague and since plaintiffs did not offer any additional arguments under the undue burden standard, the court concluded that the statute did not impose an undue burden.[134]

Defendant also appealed the District Court's severance of the auscultation provision of the statute. The Seventh Circuit performed its own undue burden analysis concerning the provision, framing the requirement such that under *Casey*, an informed consent provision must be "designed to further a legitimate state interest" and be "truthful and not misleading."[135] Accordingly, if the informed consent provision did not meet this standard, it would be an "unconstitutional burden on a woman's right to choose."[136] Therefore, the Seventh Circuit framed the "truthful and not misleading" standard as a central inquiry under the undue burden standard where informed consent provisions are concerned.

Nevertheless, unlike the District Court, the Seventh Circuit found that the provision did not impose an undue burden and was thus constitutional. The court determined that the statute provided the physician with discretion regarding whether to fully disclose the

---

Wis. Stat. Ann. § 253.10(3)(c)(1)(a-k) (West 2012), *amended by* 2011 Wis. Legis. Serv. 217 (West).

[129] *Karlin*, 975 F. Supp. at 1218.

[130] *Id.* at 1219.

[131] *Id.*

[132] Karlin v. Foust, 188 F.3d 446, 471-72 (7th Cir. 1999).

[133] *Id.* at 472, n.12.

[134] *Id.*

[135] *Id.* at 491.

[136] *Id.*

existence or non-existence of the heartbeat based on her medical knowledge.[137] Thus, the Seventh Circuit held that the provision was "truthful and not misleading," and therefore constitutional. Interestingly, the Court completely ignored the large fraction test when analyzing the informed consent provision, even though it used it in its analysis of the statute's waiting period provision.[138]

However, since the provision at issue here is not mandatory,[139] using this Article's earlier iteration of a strengthened undue burden standard would not have saved it. That is to say, a voluntary provision cannot be said to place an undue burden on a "large fraction" of the women it affects. The purpose prong analysis similarly would not have been effective here because again, the provision is voluntary. It is for forced provisions, discussed in Part IV(A)(2) below, that this reinvigorated standard will be useful.

Ultrasound provisions were not challenged again at the federal level until 2010, in *Hope Medical Group for Women v. Caldwell.*[140] In *Hope Medical,* a Fifth Circuit federal judge issued a temporary restraining order against a law that would force women to undergo and review an ultrasound before they were allowed to receive an abortion.[141] Several new laws with ultrasound requirements were introduced in 2010-2011.[142] These new laws prompted the challenge in *Hope Medical,* in addition to two other court cases: *Stuart v. Huff*

---

[137] The court determined that the statue provided the physician with discretion regarding the content of the discussion about available services depending on the length of pregnancy, and thus whether to disclose the existence or non-existence of the heartbeat based on the physician's medical knowledge.

[138] *Compare id.* at 483-88 *with id.* at 491-93.

[139] *See* WISC. STAT. ANN. § 253.10, *amended by* 2011-2012 Wisc. Legis. Serv. Act 217 (2011 S.B. § 306) (West 2012):

> (c) *Informed consent.* Except if a medical emergency exists, a woman›s consent to an abortion is informed only if all of the following first take place:
> g. That fetal ultrasound imaging and auscultation of fetal heart tone services *are available* that enable a pregnant woman to view the image or hear the heartbeat of her unborn child. In so informing the woman and describing these services, the physician shall advise the woman as to how she may obtain these services *if she desires to do so.* (Emphasis added.)

[140] *Clinics Win Injunction Against Louisiana Abortion Law:* Hope Med. Group for Women v. Caldwell, 18 No. 4 WESTLAW J. HEALTH LAW 1 (2010).

[141] *Id.*

[142] *See Laws Affecting Reproductive Health and Rights: 2011 State Policy Review,* GUTTMACHER INST., http://www.guttmacher.org/statecenter/updates/2011/statetrends42011.html (last visited Oct. 28, 2012) [hereinafter *2011 State Policy Review*].

in a North Carolina District Court, and *Texas Medical Providers Performing Abortion Services v. Lakey*, in the Fifth Circuit.

In *Stuart v. Huff*, a North Carolina District Court struck down a statute requiring a physician to perform an ultrasound at least four hours in advance of the abortion and make the images visible when describing them.[143] This is a Group D, or "speech and display" law.[144] The law was challenged under the First Amendment.[145] In their complaint, plaintiffs argued that it "compell[ed] unwilling speakers to deliver the state's message discouraging abortion."[146] Plaintiffs also argued that the law imposed an undue burden on a woman's liberty interests.[147] The defendants believed the challenge should be analyzed not under the First Amendment, but under the undue burden standard used in *Casey*.[148] The fact that supporters of the law were arguing in favor of an undue burden analysis (and against a First Amendment analysis) is a testament to the potential strength of a First Amendment challenge and indicative of the weakness of the undue burden standard.

The *Stuart* court responded to the defendants' argument by asserting that *Casey* did not combine the undue burden/liberty interest analysis with the First Amendment analysis.[149] The court noted that the undue burden standard in *Casey* was only used to evaluate the Due Process Clause challenge and that the First Amendment discussion was separate.[150] The court refused to assume that the Supreme Court in *Casey* meant to disregard the importance of First Amendment law when speech concerned abortion. Therefore, it declined to apply the undue burden analysis to the speech and display requirement.[151] Instead, the court analyzed the statute's speech

---

[143] Stuart v. Huff, 834 F. Supp. 2d 424 (M.D.N.C. 2011). The Defendants argued that women may avert their eyes and use a "technological device" to avoid hearing the description, but since they have to sign a form afterward declaring that the speech and display requirements were met, it is unclear how they would be able to tell that the women complied with the law. *Id.* at 433. *See also* N.C. GEN. STAT. ANN. § 90-21.85(a), (b) (West 2012) for the text of the statute in controversy in *Stuart*.

[144] This is terminology used to describe these laws in a succinct manner.

[145] *Stuart*, 834 F. Supp. 2d at 428.

[146] *Id.*

[147] *Id.* at 427, n.1.

[148] *Id.* at 430.

[149] *Id.*

[150] *Id.*

[151] *Id.* The court further notes that the legislation in *Casey* that most closely resembles the legislation at issue has to do with the physician informing the woman of the availability of printed materials published by the State. *Id.* at 430, n.6. The Court notes that, "[w]hat the state can say itself is very different from

and display requirement under strict scrutiny. The court found that it failed to pass strict scrutiny and struck down that portion of the Act.[152] It is unclear, however, if this means that a doctor's First Amendment right trumps a pregnant women's Fourteenth Amendment Due Process right, considering how much stronger a strict scrutiny analysis appears to be in comparison to an undue burden analysis.

However, not all courts have chosen to apply a First Amendment strict scrutiny analysis to informed consent provisions as the court did in *Stuart*. In *Texas Medical Providers Performing Abortion Services v. Lakey,* the Fifth Circuit Court of Appeals chose to analyze the state's "speech and display law" using an undue burden standard.[153] The law has similar informed consent provisions to the legislation at issue in *Stuart*, with the exception that after the ultrasound the physician is normally required to wait 24-hours before performing the abortion.[154] Nonetheless, using an undue burden analysis the court vacated the district court's grant of a preliminary injunction.[155]

The court articulated a clear rule for informed consent provisions as a whole, stating that, "informed consent laws that do not impose an undue burden on the woman's right to have an abortion are permissible if they require truthful, nonmisleading, and relevant disclosures."[156] Notably, this is different from the *Karlin* court's framing of the truthful and misleading standard as central to the undue burden analysis itself. However, since the appellees did not assert that the provision at issue in *Lakey* was an undue burden, the court did not analyze the provision under the undue burden standard, but merely assumed that the provision did not constitute an undue burden.[157]

Therefore, though the court used the term, "undue burden," it did not actually perform that analysis and instead declared that if the provision at issue was not an undue burden and if it was truthful and non-misleading, a First Amendment claim "trump[ed] the balance *Casey* struck between women's rights and the states'

---

what the state can compel individuals to say." *Id.*

[152] *Id.* at 432-33.

[153] Tex. Med. Providers Performing Abortion Servs. v. Lakey, 667 F.3d 570 (5th Cir. 2012).

[154] *See* TEX. HEALTH & SAFETY CODE ANN. § 171.012(a)(4) (West 2012).

[155] *Lakey,* 667 F.3d at 584.

[156] *Id.* at 576. The Court further declared that these laws do not fall under compelled ideological speech that would trigger First Amendment strict scrutiny. *Id.*

[157] *See id.* at 577.

prerogatives."[158] The court went on to hold that the speech and display requirements are the "epitome of truthful, non-misleading information," and are relevant to informed consent.[159] The court never gave an explanation for why it declined to actually analyze the statute under the undue burden standard when it framed this standard as a preliminary requirement. Therefore, as an example of the application of the strengthened undue burden standard, the next section is a hypothetical exploration of its application to the law at issue in *Lakey*.

2. Application of the Strengthened Undue Burden Standard to the *Lakey* Statute

If the *Lakey* court had analyzed this provision under the strengthened undue burden standard, the ultrasound issue may have been framed as: is the requirement to have an ultrasound, and hear a description of the ultrasound images, truthful and not misleading? If so, does this requirement have the purpose or effect of creating a substantial obstacle for a large fraction of the woman to whom this provision applies? If not, does the ultrasound provision, as combined with other existing restrictions on abortion in Texas law, create a substantial obstacle for a large fraction of the women to whom these restrictions apply?

The *Lakey* court was adamant that the provision at issue was the "epitome" of truth and not misleading, and thus the provision would still pass under the first prong of that analysis.[160] Therefore, the next step would be to analyze whether the restriction was enacted with the purpose of creating a substantial obstacle for women seeking an abortion or if it was intended to hinder their free choice. That may be problematic depending on how legislators have discussed the bill in public: not all legislators who oppose abortion on all grounds express their opinions publicly.[161] Additionally, pro-choice advocates may be hurting themselves under the law by noting publicly that it will not deter women from obtaining abortions.[162] However, advocating that courts go through the complete analysis

---

[158] *Id.*

[159] *Id.* at 578.

[160] *Id.*

[161] *But see supra*, note 90 to review the statement from a Mississippi representative on the legislative intent behind the state's law restricting abortion access.

[162] *See id.*

may bring to light anecdotal evidence of illegitimate purpose — that this legislation is intended to "hinder"[163] a woman's choice.

Next, the restriction should be analyzed in light of the effect it has on a large fraction of women for whom it would operate as an obstacle. This would be challenging. It may require the testimony of medical professionals regarding whether or not seeing an ultrasound and hearing the images described would actually "restrict" a woman's free choice. Moreover, there may not be a clear way to go about presenting that type of information. Lastly, courts are largely unsympathetic to emotional arguments made in opposition to abortion restrictions.[164]

Notably, one of the exceptions that applies under the statute is for survivors of sexual assault (if a *particular* pregnancy is the result of that assault). This exception only applies if a woman has reported the assault or if she "reasonably" feared "serious bodily injury" in retaliation for reporting.[165] Therefore, women who did not report because of fear of emotional abuse or non-serious bodily injury[166] are still subject to the ultrasound description. Moreover, since most survivors of assault do not report,[167] women will have to assert that they would be "reasonably" at risk of "serious bodily injury" if they were to report, thus abrogating their autonomy to make the best and safest decision for themselves regarding reporting. However, when analyzed from the perspective of a pregnant

---

[163] *See* Planned Parenthood of Se. Pa. v. Casey, 505 U.S. 833, 877 (1992).

[164] *See supra* note 108.

[165] *See* TEX. HEALTH & SAFETY CODE ANN. § 171.012(a)(5) (West 2012). It is notable that if the abortion is at or before seven weeks, the required ultrasound is a transvaginal probe rather than the traditional abdominal ultrasound. This means that survivors of trauma, specifically those who have been raped, will be subject to the law if they cannot prove that they still have a reasonable fear of serious bodily injury.

[166] And who is defining "serious bodily injury?" It is not listed in the definitions portion of the statute. *See* TEX. HEALTH & SAFETY CODE ANN. § 171.002 (West 2012).

[167] *See* California Coalition Against Sexual Assault, 2008 REPORT: RESEARCH ON RAPE AND VOLENCE 6 (2008), *available at* http://www.ncdsv.org/images/CAL-CASA_ResearchOnRapeAndViolenceReport_2008.pdf ("Only 16 % of rapes are ever reported to the police."); *Domestic Violence Facts*, NAT'L COALITION AGAINST DOMESTIC VIOLENCE (July 2007), http://www.ncadv.org/files/DomesticViolenceFactSheet(National).pdf ("Most cases of domestic violence are never reported to the police.") (citing MURRAY A. STRAUS, RICHARD J. GELLES, & CHRISTINE SMITH, PHYSICAL VIOLENCE IN AMERICAN FAMILIES: RISK FACTORS AND ADAPTATIONS TO VIOLENCE IN 8,145 FAMILIES 486 (1990) (concluding that "reports to police [are] the exception rather than the rule. Only 6.7% of all husband-to-wife assaults are reported to police.").

woman in a relationship wherein she is experiencing emotional abuse or non-serious bodily injury, it is possible that this provision may fail the large fraction test. In other words, a large portion of pregnant women in abusive relationships may be precluded from reporting due to this provision and therefore denied the opportunity to opt-out of the ultrasound description. In fact, advocates could potentially analogize to some of the same facts used in the *Casey* opinion when that court struck down the husband notification provision under the undue burden test.[168]

Finally, advocates should analyze the ultrasound provision in the context of other existing provisions in Texas that restrict abortion, and determine whether these combined restrictions would amount to a substantial obstacle.

B. *Fetal Pain Laws*

The second most common group of informed consent provisions are those that proscribe an abortion after 20 weeks due to studies that suggest that this is the point at which the fetus can feel pain.[169] These studies are widely contested in the medical community.[170] When making and passing these laws, legislators typically reference studies that show hyperexcitability in fetal responses to stimulus.[171] However, medical professionals cite the problem of using stimulus responses to pain as evidence of the actual feeling of pain for two reasons: (1) the fetus has not developed the necessary

---

[168] *See Casey*, 505 U.S. at 895.

[169] *See, e.g.*, ALA. CODE 1975 § 26-23B-2 (West, current through end of the 2012 Regular and 1st special Sessions); IND. CODE ANN. §16-34-1-9 (West, current with all 2012 legislation); IDAHO CODE ANN. § 18-503 (West, current through end of 2012 2nd Regular Session of the 61st legislature); KAN. CODE ANN. § 65-6722 (West, current through 2012 regular session); 2012 La. Sess. Law Serv. Act 738 (S.B. 766) (West, 2012); NEB. REV. ST. § 28-3, 104 (West, current through the 102nd Legislature Second Regular Session 2012); 63 OKL. ST. ANN. § 1-745.3 (West, current through September 2012); Unborn Child Pain Awareness Act of 2006, H.R. 6099, 109th Cong. (2006) (this law was not passed, but provides an example of the discussion at the federal level). Most of these statutes are titled something along the lines of "Pain-Capable Unborn Child Protection Act," and they all seem to be modeled after each other.

[170] *See, e.g.*, ROYAL COLLEGE OF OBSTETRICIANS AND GYNAECOLOGISTS, FETAL AWARENESS: REVIEW OF RESEARCH AND RECOMMENDATIONS FOR PRACTICE (2010), *available at* http://www.rcog.org.uk/files/rcog-corp/RCOGFetalAwareness-WPR0610.pdf.

[171] *See* note 169, *supra*.

cortical structures for feeling pain and (2) pain is largely conceived as a multi-faceted response.[172]

Therefore, while anti-choice activists equate responses to stimulus as capacity to feel pain, this is a complicated assumption. The capacity to respond to stimulus exists before the brain/injury connection has happened in the fetus, and therefore it is impossible for nerve responses to physical injury to travel from the injury situs to the brain itself, communicating "pain." Moreover, analgesic practitioners conceptualize pain as "biopsychosocial," an experience informed not just by the senses, but by emotional components as well.[173] Additionally, movement of the kind cited by advocates of fetal pain statutes can also be found in patients who are in vegetative states—that is, there is proof that the body naturally reacts to certain stimulus even when the necessary pain structures no longer exist.[174]

Nonetheless, seven states have enacted laws banning abortion after 20 weeks,[175] explicitly justifying the bans based on reference to studies that indicate that the fetus can feel pain at 20 weeks.[176]

---

[172] *See generally* Stuart W.G. Derbyshire, 13(1) Bioethics 1, 16-28 (1999) (describing EEG measurements of responses to noxious stimuli throughout fetal life as compared to adult life, and concluding that the fetus lacks the necessary biological and contextual development to experience pain).

[173] *See id* at 4.

[174] *See* Tobin, *supra* note 91, at 145-46.

[175] While Arizona's codified law says twenty weeks, this state's fetal pain law actually bans abortion after twenty weeks of gestation or only eighteen weeks post-fertilization. Other states' laws are twenty weeks post-fertilization. Robin Marty, *Arizona Governor Jan Brewer Signs Country's First 20-Week Gestational Ban Into Law*, RH Reality Check (April 12, 2012, 9:42 PM), http://www.rhrealitycheck.org/article/2012/04/12/arizona-governor-jan-brewer-signs-countrys-first-20-week-gestational-ban-into-law. For a list of the statutes, *see* note 169, *supra*.

[176] These states are: Alabama, Arizona, Idaho, Indiana, Kansas, Nebraska, and Oklahoma. Additionally, eleven states (Arkansas, Arizona, Georgia, Indiana, Louisiana, Minnesota, Missouri, Oklahoma, South Dakota, Texas, and Utah) require mandated counseling that includes information on fetal pain. Arizona, Oklahoma, Minnesota, and Utah only require this information after twenty weeks, and Missouri only after twenty-two weeks. *Overview of Abortion Laws, supra* note 93. While Oklahoma and Arizona ban abortion after twenty weeks, they still have an exception for the life and health of the mother, which means their fetal pain counseling provision doesn't go into effect unless that exception applies. Fetal pain-based informed consent statutes typically use language such as the following:

> By 20 weeks' gestation, the unborn child has the physical structures necessary to experience pain. There is evidence that by 20 weeks' gestation unborn children seek to evade certain stimuli in a manner which in an infant or an adult would be interpreted to be a response

Abortion rights advocates, however, have been reluctant to challenge legislation related to fetal pain.[177]

The first case challenging a fetal pain ban was brought in Idaho in September of 2011, and was recently decided.[178] In that case, an Idaho woman, Jennie Linn McCormack, procured a medical abortifacient over the internet.[179] She was subsequently charged by the Bannock County prosecutor in Idaho for undergoing an abortion in a manner unauthorized by statute, a felony.[180] She challenged the criminal charges and she also argued that she had standing to challenge enforcement of Idaho's fetal pain ban (dubbed the *Pain-Capable Unborn Child Protection Act*, or PUCPA), which proscribes abortions after 20 weeks.[181] The court ruled that McCormack was likely to succeed on the merits in challenging the statute that criminalized women procuring unauthorized abortions because it imposed an undue burden.[182] Though the court ruled that McCormack did not have standing to challenge PUCPA, it did indicate that PUCPA might be found to impose an undue burden if challenged by someone with standing.[183]

The only other case dealing with fetal pain in connection with informed consent came before a federal court in June of 2011. In

---

to pain. Anesthesia is routinely administered to unborn children who are 20 weeks' gestational age or older who undergo prenatal surgery.
Tobin, *supra* note 91, at 113-14 (citing Ga. Code Ann. § 31-9A-4(a)(3) (West 2006); *see also* Ark. Code Ann. § 20-16-1105(a)(1)(A) (West 2005); Okla. Stat. Ann. tit. 63, § 1-738.10(A) (West Supp. 2008); La. Rev. Stat. Ann. § 40:1299.35.6(D)(3)(a)(ii) (West 2001)).

[177] *See* Kathryn Smith, *Abortion-Rights Groups Absent on Fetal Pain Laws*, Politico (Aug. 13, 2012, 4:29PM), http://www.politico.com/news/stories/0812/79681.html.

[178] Rebecca Boone, *Idaho Doctor-Lawyer Fights Fetal Pain Law*, The Associated Press (April 17, 2012, 10:53 AM), http://www.washingtontimes.com/news/2012/apr/17/idaho-doctor-lawyer-fights-fetal-pain-abortion-law/?page=all.

[179] McCormack v. Heideman, 2012 U.S. App. LEXIS 19051 *1, *4-5.

[180] *Id.*

[181] *Id.* at *9.

[182] *Id.* at *35. The court said that this statute required women to police their providers' compliance with Idaho regulations. *Id.* at *28. The court went on to include a remarkably detailed discussion of why women choose abortion, and the existing obstacles they already face. *Id.* at *28-35. This is perhaps the most supportive language ever used by a Circuit court regarding a woman's choice to terminate a pregnancy. However, the court narrowed the preliminary injunction to only enjoin future prosecution of McCormack, but broadened it to include all sections of the law (therefore including all trimesters). *See id.* at *41, 47.

[183] *Id.* at *49-50 ("PUCPA was not enacted without controversy. Idaho's own Attorney General explained in a 17-page letter that PUCPA 'plainly

Planned Parenthood of Indiana v. Commissioner of the Indiana State Department of Health,[184] the court used only a First Amendment analysis regarding physician speech, rather than using the undue burden standard as a parallel determinative of whether "fetal pain" additions to informed consent legislation constituted an undue burden.[185] The court, however, did find that discussion of fetal pain by physicians met compelled speech standards under the First Amendment.[186]

Planned Parenthood of Indiana is similar to *Lakey*. Thus, the proposed strengthened undue burden standard should be a parallel analysis to the First Amendment challenge. In addition, advocates involved in our hypothetical Lakey case might be able to win since the science surrounding fetal pain can be "false, misleading, and irrelevant" according to the court in *Planned Parenthood of Indiana*.[187] Misleading is the very opposite of the preliminary "truthful and not misleading"[188] inquiry in the strengthened undue burden standard and statutes regarding fetal pain would thus fail.

Additionally, the Idaho fetal pain 20-week gestational ban, if challenged by someone with standing, may come out differently under the strengthened undue burden standard. The Idaho statute's 20-week gestational ban includes women who have late-term diagnoses of fetal abnormalities. A 20-week ban could be shown to pose a substantial obstacle to those women's choices. However, the hypothetical plaintiff would still have to overcome the state's ability to proscribe abortion after viability. If Idaho can show that a fetus can be viable after 20 weeks, the undue burden test becomes obsolete because the state has the right to ban abortions. On the other hand, if Idaho fails to prove that a fetus is viable after 20 weeks, the statute would likely fail under the undue burden standard, since it is clear that the purpose of the statute is to hinder a woman's choice, and it is also clear that it places a substantial obstacle in the path

---

intends to erect a substantial obstacle to the right to choose,' and 'there is strong reason to believe that [PUCPA] is unconstitutional under existing precedent.''). I argue that by mentioning these facts even though they were not necessary to the standing analysis, the Court implies it would be likely to overturn PUCPA if someone with standing brought a challenge.

[184] Planned Parenthood of Ind. v. Comm'r of the Ind. State Dept. of Health, 794 F. Supp. 2d 892 (S.D. Ind. 2011).

[185] This is because the law was not challenged under the undue burden standard, but rather under the First Amendment. *See id.* at 914-21.

[186] *Id.* at 919-21.

[187] *Id.* at 920.

[188] Planned Parenthood of Se. Pa. v. Casey, 505 U.S. 833, 882 (1992).

of women seeking abortions after 20 weeks.[189] It would certainly be a concern for those litigating such a case that the court would find that a fetus can be viable after 20 weeks, setting a new precedent for 20-week bans all across the country.

V. WHAT IS NEXT FOR THE UNDUE BURDEN STANDARD?

If courts continue down the path they have taken in recent years with the undue burden standard, it seems that there are very few abortion restrictions that would ruled unconstitutional if challenged. The pro-life movement is knowledgeable in crafting laws that simultaneously hinder a woman's choice and yet somehow escape invalidation under the standard. The increased number of restrictive statutes enacted in the last three years is a byproduct of this increased legislative savvy.[190] Moreover, the undue burden standard's weakness leaves the pro-choice movement afraid to litigate too many challenges, lest bad precedent embolden conservative legislators in other states to enact similar restrictions.

The undue burden standard is unique as a separate and more burdensome standard for challenged fundamental rights. It seems clear that the Court in *Casey* was attempting to balance public opinion on the issue, but in doing so, removed some of *Roe's* protections around the right to choose. Despite its unclear application, it is unlikely that the United States Supreme Court will completely do away with the undue burden standard. However, its inconsistent use by lower federal courts calls for clarification. The standard needs to be strengthened by re-emphasizing the purpose prong and the large fraction test as inquiries that must be included each time the standard is applied. Moreover, advocates should always raise the standard in challenges where an abortion restriction is at issue, including challenging the law on the basis that all the abortion restrictions in the given state combine to create an undue burden.

---

[189] *See* McCormack v. Heideman, 2012 U.S. App. LEXIS 19051 at *49-50 ("PUCPA was not enacted without controversy. Idaho's own Attorney General explained in a 17-page letter that PUCPA 'plainly intends to erect a substantial obstacle to the right to choose,' and 'there is strong reason to believe that [PUCPA] is unconstitutional under existing precedent.").

[190] *See* 2011 State Policy Review, *supra* note 142.

www.ingramcontent.com/pod-product-compliance
Lightning Source LLC
Chambersburg PA
CBHW031947190326
41519CB00007B/706